General editor: Graham Handley MA PH D

Brodie's Notes on William Shakespeare's

# Richard III

D1824253

Kenneth Hardacre MA
Formerly Head of English, Queens' School, Bushey

**Pan Books** London and Sydney

This revised edition published 1985 by Pan Books Ltd
Cavaye Place, London SW10 9PG
10 9 8 7 6 5 4 3 2 1
© Kenneth Hardacre 1985
ISBN 0 330 50196 8
Photoset by Parker Typesetting Service, Leicester
Printed and bound in Great Britain by
Richard Clay (The Chaucer Press) Ltd, Bungay, Suffolk

# Contents

Line references in these Notes are to the
*Arden Shakespeare: Richard III*,
but as references are also given to particular acts
and scenes, the Notes may be used with any
edition of the play.

# Preface

This student revision aid is based on the principle that in any close examination of Shakespeare's plays 'the text's the thing'. Seeing a performance, or listening to a tape or record of a performance, is essential and is in itself a valuable and stimulating experience in understanding and appreciation. However, a real evaluation of Shakespeare's greatness, of his universality and of the nature of his literary and dramatic art, can only be achieved by constant application to the texts of the plays themselves. These revised editions of Brodie's Notes are intended to supplement that process through detailed critical commentary.

The first aim of each book is to fix the whole play in the reader's mind by providing a concise summary of the plot, relating it back, where appropriate, to its source or sources. Subsequently the book provides a summary of each scene, followed by *critical comments*. These may convey its importance in the dramatic structure of the play, creation of atmosphere, indication of character development, significance of figurative language etc, and they will also explain or paraphrase difficult words or phrases and identify meaningful references. At the end of each act revision questions are set to test the student's specific and broad understanding and appreciation of the play.

An extended critical commentary follows this scene by scene analysis. This embraces such major elements as characterization, imagery, the use of blank verse and prose, soliloquies and other aspects of the play which the editor considers need close attention. The paramount aim is to send the reader back to the text. The book concludes with a series of revision questions which require a detailed knowledge of the play; the first of these has notes by the editor of what *might* be included in a written answer. The intention is to stimulate and to guide; the whole emphasis of this commentary is to encourage the student's *involvement* in the play, to develop disciplined critical responses and thus promote personal enrichment through the imaginative experience of our greatest writer.

Graham Handley

# Shakespeare and the Elizabethan Playhouse

William Shakespeare was born in Stratford-upon-Avon in 1564, and there are reasons to suppose that he came from a relatively prosperous family. He was probably educated at Stratford Grammar School and, at the age of eighteen, married Anne Hathaway, who was twenty-six. They had three children, a girl born shortly after their marriage, followed by twins in 1585 (the boy died in 1596). It seems likely that Shakespeare left for London shortly after a company of visiting players had visited Stratford in 1585, for by 1592 – according to the jealous testimony of one of his fellow-writers, Robert Greene – he was certainly making his way both as actor and dramatist. The theatres were closed because of the plague in 1593, but when they reopened Shakespeare worked with the Lord Chamberlain's men, later the King's men, and became a shareholder in each of the two theatres with which he was most closely associated, the Globe and the Blackfriars. He later purchased New Place, a considerable property in his home town of Stratford, to which he retired in 1611; there he entertained his great contemporary Ben Jonson (1572–1637) and the poet Michael Drayton (1563–1631). An astute businessman, he lived comfortably in the town until his death in 1616.

This is a very brief outline of the life of our greatest writer, for little more can be said of him with certainty, though the plays – and poems – are living witness to the wisdom, humanity and many-faceted nature of the man. He was both popular and successful as a dramatist, perhaps less so as an actor. He probably began work as a dramatist in the late 1580s, by collaborating with other playwrights and adapting old plays, and by 1598 Francis Meres was paying tribute to his excellence in both comedy and tragedy. His first original play was probably *Love's Labour's Lost* (1590), and while the theatres were closed during the plague he wrote his narrative poems, *Venus and Adonis* (1593) and *The Rape of Lucrece* (1594). The sonnets were almost certainly written in the 1590s though not published until 1609; the first 126 are addressed to a young man who was his friend and patron, while the rest are concerned with the 'dark lady'.

The dating of Shakespeare's plays has exercised scholars ever since the publication of the First Folio (1623) listed them as comedies, histories and tragedies. It seems more important to look at them as far as possible chronologically, in order to trace Shakespeare's considerable development as a dramatist. The first period, say to the middle of the 1590s, included such plays as *Love's Labour's Lost, The Comedy of Errors, Richard III, The Taming of the Shrew, Romeo and Juliet* and *Richard II*. These early plays embrace the categories listed in the First Folio, so that Shakespeare the craftsman is evident in his capacity for variety of subject and treatment. The next phase includes *A Midsummer Night's Dream, The Merchant of Venice, Henry IV Parts I and II, Henry V* and *Much Ado About Nothing*, as well as *Julius Caesar, As You Like It* and *Twelfth Night*. These are followed, in the early years of the century, by his great tragic period, *Hamlet, Othello, King Lear* and *Macbeth*, with *Antony and Cleopatra* and *Coriolanus* belonging to 1607–09. The final phase embraces the romances (1610–13), *Cymbeline, The Tempest* and *The Winter's Tale* and the historical play *Henry VIII*.

Each of these revision aids will place the individual text under examination in the chronology of the remarkable dramatic output which thus spanned twenty years from the early 1590s to about 1613.

At the time of Shakespeare there were probably not more than five public theatres in the land, all in London, and they were built according to the design of the inn-yards of the period, which had been found marvellously convenient places for the presentation of plays. The theatre was circular or octagonal in shape. The main part of the auditorium was the large round pit, open to the sky, in whch the poorer people *stood* (the 'groundlings'). Encircling this, round the walls, were three balconies, covered on top but not in front (like the 'stands' on a football ground), and containing seats. The price of admission to the pit was one penny, while proportionately higher charges were made for balcony seats, according to their position. When it was wet the performance was postponed until the next day.

The stage was large, and this made it easy to show crowd and battle scenes, which are frequent in Elizabethan drama. It even allowed for the placing of the tents of Richard and Richmond, one on either side of the stage, in Act V, Scene 3. It jutted far into the pit; hence it made no difference that people stood at the

side of the stage as well as in front. The fact that the actors had their audience on three sides of them had three important consequences.

First, elaborate scenery was not practicable, although movable properties like a bed or a throne would give some slight indication of the setting. The scenery was created in the imagination of the audience by the words of the characters in the play and by natural touches in the dialogue. Notice, for example, how Queen Elizabeth's words at the end of IV, 1 not only call attention to the setting, before the Tower, but also bring out the pathos of the situation.

Secondly, the speaking of soliloquies and asides when the performers were closely surrounded by their audience seemed much more natural than in the modern theatre. This is a point of considerable importance in a play like *Richard III*, which contains so many soliloquies in which Richard outlines his plans, as though confiding in the audience, and so many asides in which he comments on the situation.

Thirdly, the play could go straight on without intervals, and frequent changes of scene were immaterial. Consequently, a succession of different settings, as in Act III, is quite common in Elizabethan drama. In a play with changes of scenery the audience would become impatient at the constant delays. At the present time there is a return to a simple stage setting, in keeping with that of Shakespeare's day, as, for instance, at the Royal Shakespeare Theatre. There is good reason to believe that Shakespeare's plays took considerably less time to perform than they do today. The Prologue to *Romeo and Juliet,* for instance, refers to 'the two hours' traffic of our stage', though this could hardly apply to *all* plays. *Richard III* is unusually long, with over 3400 lines.

In the absence of curtains the end of a scene was frequently marked by rhyming lines (e.g. I,1; I,2; I,4). The rhyming couplets at the end of the Duchess of York's speech in IV,4 are intended to show the end of an episode (the scene goes on to deal with Richard's attempts to win over Queen Elizabeth), and this obviously applies also to the rhyming couplets of the scene at Bosworth Field (V,3). What seems the end of only part of a scene as printed in our editions may well have appeared the end of a separate incident to Shakespeare, for he did not divide his plays into acts and scenes (see p.20). Conversely, by means of unbroken continuity, Shakespeare could obtain effects which are often lost in the modern theatre where there are breaks between the scenes. One such effect is Queen Margaret's soliloquy at the beginning of IV,4, which provides a significant comment if it *immediately* follows Richard's words at the end of the previous scene. The Quarto texts of *Richard III* are quite undivided.

Just as the scenery had to be *put into* the play, so had entrances and exits to be arranged as *part* of the play. Today an actor can get into position before the rise of the curtain, but on the open stage it would seem artificial if he walked on and then started his first speech, or finished the scene and then walked off. Shakespeare often makes it clear that his characters are in the middle of a conversation as they enter (e.g. II,1; II,4; IV,5), and Lady Anne's words at the beginning of I,2 provide a natural opening for the scene that follows. Such endings as II,4, 'Go; I'll conduct you to the sanctuary', clear the stage and at the same time fit in perfectly naturally with the play. It follows that dead bodies always had to be carried off the stage as part of the action of the play. After Clarence has been stabbed in I,4, the murderer drags the body off the stage, saying, 'I'll drown you in the malmsey-butt within'. Richard may well be killed off stage, and Professor Dover Wilson points out how effective is Richard's famous cry for a horse for a general entering on foot in a battle scene, since a stage-entry on horseback was impracticable.

It was not unknown for the stage floor to be equipped with a trap-door for the sudden appearance and disappearance of ghosts and spirits, and some theatres had a flying apparatus by which such could descend on the stage with the aid of ropes on runners. It is not clear how the ghosts of V,3 would enter.

At the back of the stage was a recess 'within', and this was curtained and could be shut off when desired. Shakespeare seems to have made no use of this inner stage in *Richard III*, unless Hastings comes forward from the inner stage when the messenger knocks at his door in III,2.

Above the recess was a balcony, which served for an upper room, castle walls and such scenes. This, too, could be curtained off. This was used in III,7, where the original stage-direction says, 'Enter Richard aloft, between two Bishops.'

People who wanted to be in the public eye were able to hire stools actually on the stage itself. Payment of one shilling extra entitled them to have their pipes lighted by a page, thus showing to all and sundry that they were in a position to be attended. Such a privilege would be valued by country gentlemen who wanted it to be known that they had come up to town. It was a source of continual annoyance to playwrights that actors 'gagged' in order to please these aristocratic playgoers.

Women were not allowed to act by law. Consequently women's parts had to be taken by boys with unbroken voices. The ban on actresses accounts for the few women's parts in plays of the period, though some were always introduced for the sake of variety. It also accounts for the large number of plays where a woman disguises herself as a page boy.

Plays were not acted in period costume, though frequently *some* attempt was made to suggest a period, and the result must often have been a bizarre compromise. Thus all Shakespeare's plays can be said to have been first acted in 'modern dress'. Although there was no scenery, managers spared no expense on the most lavish of costumes.

On days when the theatre was open a flag was flown from the turret, and when the play was about to begin a trumpet was sounded. The turret of the Globe Theatre housed a big alarum bell, a favourite theatrical effect. This bell would ring out the alarums for battle and retreat. Perhaps it would lend more impressiveness to Shakespeare's flimsy battle scene.

Shakespeare and his contemporaries often adapted their plays from sources in history and literature, extending an incident or a myth, or creating a dramatic narrative from known facts. They were always aware of their own audiences, and frequently included topical references, sometimes of a satirical flavour, which would appeal to – and be understood by – the groundlings as well as their wealthier patrons who occupied the boxes. Shakespeare obviously learned much from his fellow-dramatists and actors, being on good terms with many of them. Ben Jonson paid generous tribute to him in the lines prefaced to the First Folio of Shakespeare's plays:

Thou art a monument without a tomb,
And art alive still, while thy book doth live
And we have wits to read, and praise to give.

Among his contemporaries were Thomas Kyd (1558–94) and Christopher Marlowe (1564–93). Kyd wrote *The Spanish Tragedy*,

the revenge motif here foreshadowing the much more sophis-
ticated treatment evident in *Hamlet,* while Marlowe evolved the
'mighty line' of blank verse, a combination of natural speech and
elevated poetry. The quality and variety of Shakespeare's blank
verse owes something to the innovatory brilliance of Marlowe,
but it is imbued with the stamp of individuality, richness of
associations, technical virtuosity and, above all, the genius of
imaginative power. The texts of Shakespeare's plays are still
mines for scholars, and the editors of these revision aids have
used the Arden editions of Shakespeare, which are regarded as
pre-eminent for their scholarly approach. They are strongly
recommended for advanced students, but other editions, like
The New Penguin Shakespeare, The New Swan, The Signet are
all good annotated editions currently available. A reading list of
selected reliable works on the play being studied is provided at
the end of the book, and students are advised to turn to this as
their interest in the play deepens.

# Literary terms used in this study aid

**Antithesis** A form of words in which thought or expression is balanced by contrast. E.g. 'Hath dimm'd your infant morn to aged night.'

**Conceit** An over-fanciful metaphor, an exaggerated image, usually developed at some length. E.g. II,2, 68–70.

**Dramatic irony** This arises from the difference between the situation in the play as known to the audience and as supposed by the characters (or by some of them). The basis of dramatic irony is ambiguity of meaning. A remark by one character may have a surface meaning for the other characters but an additional significance for the audience.

**Hyperbole** This figure of speech uses deliberately exaggerated statement which is not intended to be taken literally. Its purpose is to express deep feeling or to produce a strong impression. E.g. 'The most arch deed of piteous massacre/That ever yet this land was guilty of.'

**Metaphor** Whereas in a simile two things are compared, in a metaphor the name (or action or quality) of one is transferred to the other. E.g. 'I was a pack-horse in his great affairs.'

**Oxymoron** This figure of speech brings together contradictory terms in order to give extra point or emphasis. E.g. 'a living death'.

**Simile** A figure of speech in which, for emphasis or effect, two unlike things are compared introduced by 'like' or 'as'. E.g. 'like dumb statues'.

**Sticomythia** A device adopted from Greek classical drama, where a disputation or argument is carried on by 'the rapid interchange of studied repartee', characterized by antithesis and rhetorical repetition. Each speaker takes up the opponent's words, often with rather strained parallelism and word-play. E.g. IV,4 212–19 and 343–67.

# The play
## Plot, sources, treatment

### Plot

*Richard III* continues the story of the three parts of *Henry VI*. Nearly all its important characters appeared in the earlier plays of the sequence. This play deals with the last stage of the rivalry between the houses of Lancaster and York and opens as England is enjoying a period of uneasy peace under Edward IV, after the Battle of Tewkesbury and the death of Henry VI.

Richard, Duke of Gloucester and youngest brother of the King, has arranged the imprisonment of another brother, the Duke of Clarence. He plans to have Clarence murdered, to marry Lady Anne and to gain the throne on the death of the sick Edward. He woos Anne successfully, causes dissension among the Queen's relations and has Clarence murdered.

When Edward dies, Richard, with the help of the Duke of Buckingham, gains control of the young King Edward V and his brother, the Duke of York. He overcomes opposition by arresting and later executing Rivers, Grey, Vaughan and Hastings, and, by hoodwinking the Lord Mayor and citizens of London and declaring Edward IV's children illegitimate, Richard gains the crown for himself. He decides to murder the Princes, and when Buckingham hesitates to give his support he is discarded. While opposition begins to crystallize around the figure of the Earl of Richmond in Brittany, Richard plans to strengthen his position by marrying Edward IV's daughter, Elizabeth. Richmond lands in Wales with an army and the two forces meet at Bosworth. On the eve of battle the ghosts of all Richard's victims appear, prophesying success for Richmond and defeat and death for Richard. Though the latter fights with superhuman courage, he is eventually killed and the victorious Richmond announces that his marriage with Elizabeth will put an end to the dissensions of York and Lancaster.

As a commentary on the story of Richard's progress through blood to the crown and of his ultimate downfall, Shakespeare introduces the almost supernatural figure of Queen Margaret, widow of Henry VI, who pronounces curses upon the enemies of the house of York and prophesies the doom of Richard.

Historically, the action of the play covers fourteen years,

between the Battle of Tewkesbury in May 1471, and the Battle of Bosworth in August 1485.

## Sources

The three parts of Shakespeare's *Henry VI* (if they *are* all the work of Shakespeare) and his *Richard III* present a view of 15th century England which was very much the official Tudor view. Writing during the reign of Elizabeth Tudor, Shakespeare naturally adopted the details of events, their general pattern and the main lines of their interpretation from historians who themselves based their writing on accounts which were originally Tudor propaganda, written from the point of view of Henry VII (the Richmond of this play), sometimes at that king's wish, and with the express purpose of denigrating the character and achievements of Richard, who is portrayed as a monster and a tyrant, 'born under a hostile star and perishing like Antichrist'.

About 1513 Sir Thomas More wrote *The History of King Richard the Third,* and presented Richard as the supreme example of the Bad Prince, an example to be avoided by any ruler. More's Richard was a hunchback, evil from the moment of his birth; he was responsible for the death of Henry VI and of his own brother, Clarence; and was plotting for the crown long before the death of Edward IV.

In 1534 Polydore Vergil completed the first part of his *Anglica Historia,* written at the request of Henry VIII to justify the Tudors. Vergil was the first historian to introduce a pattern of ideas and interpretation into the events of the previous hundred years of English history, an interpretation which is sometimes known as the 'Tudor myth'. According to this view, Henry IV's usurpation and the death of Richard II 'broke the divine concord of society'; after Henry V's early death, a necessary expiation of the curse upon the usurping house of Lancaster, England was plunged into a civil war which culminated in the monstrous and bloody reign of Richard III, from which the country was rescued by Henry Tudor, the instrument of God's justice and vengeance, who overthrew Richard and re-established peace, concord and plenty by uniting the white rose and the red.

All this is of great relevance to Shakespeare's history plays and to *Richard III* in particular, for to a dramatist events must have a pattern, and Shakespeare largely took over the pattern which his own age found in the immediate past. The actual material for his Histories he obtained from two important Tudor works: *The Union of the Two Noble and Illustre Families of Lancaster and York* (1548), by Edward Hall, which crystallizes the Tudor tradition and 'exaggerates and hallows More's portrait and Vergil's pattern'; and the *Chronicles of England, Scotland and Ireland* (first published in 1578, with a second edition, used by Shakespeare in 1587), by Raphael Holinshed and others, which follows Hall closely, both in content and in language.

Shakespeare in turn followed Hall and Holinshed very closely, but in writing *Richard III* and his other Histories he made many alterations and several additions, and completely recast events into dramatic form, sometimes treating his sources with great freedom, so as to provide unity of plot and to create interesting characters.

From one other source Shakespeare may have derived some details concerning Clarence's dream, his murder and the prophecy about one whose name begins with G. This was *A Mirror for Magistrates*, a very popular work which appeared in several editions between 1559 and 1563 and consisted of a series of 'tragedies', stories in verse by various authors recounting the downfall of twenty eminent figures in English history, to serve as 'mirrors' or warnings. One story tells how Clarence 'was by his brother King Edward wrongfully imprisoned and by his brother Richard miserably murdered'. But though Shakespeare may have borrowed some details from *A Mirror for Magistrates*, I,4 is invented by him.

### Treatment

The following are examples of Shakespeare's chief alterations to the material he derived from his sources.

The duration of time is compressed. The whole historical sequence covered by *Richard III* was actually fourteen years. The funeral of Henry VI took place in 1471; Clarence was imprisoned in 1478; Edward IV died in 1483 – all these events are telescoped into the first six scenes. For much of the remainder of the play Shakespeare follows the sequence of events fairly closely, until after Richard's coronation. Buckingham's rebellion began in 1483; Richmond made an unsuccessful attempt at invasion in the same year; two years later he made a second attempt and landed in Wales – these events are condensed into little more than a hundred lines of IV,4.

Historical facts are altered. Queen Margaret died in France in

1482, a year before the death of Edward IV; Shakespeare makes her survive three years longer, so that her curses and their fulfilment may provide an important thread in the plot. The ages of the Duchess of York and George Stanley are altered (the one made much older, the other much younger) for dramatic purposes. Unlike More and the chroniclers, Shakespeare makes Richard deliberately plan the death of Clarence. Clarence's wife was not alive at the time of his death: she had died some time before. At the time of the Yorkist reconciliation (II,2) Richard was fighting in Scotland, Rivers was at Ludlow and Buckingham in Wales. Shakespeare also takes liberties with characters who are only referred to or who play very minor parts in the play. He makes the Earl of Rutland much younger than he really was; the son of Clarence was only three years old in 1483; the daughter of Clarence, whom Richard 'meanly match'd in marriage', did not in fact marry for another ten years.

Many scenes are completely invented by Shakespeare – for example, Richard's wooing of Anne (I,2), Clarence's dream and his murder (I,4), the visit of the members of the house of York to the Tower (IV,1), the lamentations of Margaret, Elizabeth and the Duchess of York, and Richard's wooing of Elizabeth for her daughter (IV,4), Buckingham's last speech (V,1) and Richmond's speech to his supporters at Tamworth (V,2).

Many scenes are based on information in the sources, but with the material considerably rearranged – for example, the scene at Lord Hastings's house (III,3), and the scene in which Richard, after his coronation, tests Buckingham and plans with Tyrrel the murder of the princes (IV,2).

Many scenes are built up out of mere sentences or hints in the chronicles – for example, the scenes with the citizens and the scrivener (II,3 and III,6), the second scene at Baynard's Castle (III,7), and the visits of the ghosts and Richard's account of his dream (V,3).

Above all, the character of Richard himself, although it obviously owes much to More, is amplified and almost recreated by Shakespeare, who is entirely responsible for the gaiety, the engaging cynicism, the mock piety, the bustling activity and the glee with which Richard carries out his plans.

# The text of *Richard III*

Few readers of Shakespeare realize the difficulties scholars have
had to overcome in order to establish accurate texts of the plays.
The First Folio, the first collected edition of his plays, contained
thirty-six plays and was published in 1623. Other collected editions or Folios were published in the seventeenth century, the
Third and Fourth Folios containing seven additional plays, none
of which, with the exception of *Pericles,* is now thought to be by
Shakespeare. Sixteen of the plays had already been published
separately as Quartos before 1623, and in the case of some plays,
for example *Hamlet,* more than one Quarto edition exists. Some
of these Quartos are almost word for word the same as the texts
in the First Folio and were possibly set up from Shakespeare's
own manuscript or at least from accurate theatre copies; but
others are shortened, inferior versions, possibly 'pirated' editions published by some unauthorized person who had access to
theatre copies or parts of them. It is thought that the texts of the
First Folio were set up from the good Quartos and from good
theatre copies. But these texts must all be compared, printers'
mistakes and other interference traced, before a reliable text can
be arrived at. The first editor to attempt the problem of the text
was Nicholas Rowe (1674–1718), who also divided most of the
plays into acts and scenes, supplied indications of entrances and
exits, and lists of dramatis personae, which are absent from
many of the texts in the Quarto and Folio editions. The First
Folio text of *Richard III,* however, has all the Act divisions as
continued in modern texts, and most of the scenes are given too.

The problems connected with the text of *Richard III* are
among the most difficult in all Shakespeare. The first Quarto
was published in 1597 and is now believed to have been com-
piled from the actors' memories of their parts. This was followed
by six other Quarto editions before the First Folio appeared in
1623, and there are many variations between all these texts.
There are about 32 lines in the first Quarto which do not appear
in the Folio text, and the latter contains about 200 lines which
are not in the Quarto. There is in addition a host of minor
variations and alterations – for example, in the first 82 lines of
I,4 there are nearly 70 variant readings. There have been
several theories to account for these variations, and the student

will find that modern editions of *Richard III* differ slightly. The text adopted in this study aid is that of the Arden Shakespeare, but significant variations in other editions have been commented on in the textual notes.

Although *Richard III* has always been one of the most popular of all Shakespeare's plays, for a period of over 150 years audiences were accustomed to seeing it in a version which was very different from Shakespeare's original and which even threatened to replace it. In 1700 the poet, playwright and actor, Colley Cibber, produced a version of the play which omitted entirely the parts of Queen Margaret, Edward IV, Clarence, Hastings and Queen Elizabeth's relations, and consequently the scenes which contain the dream and murder of Clarence (I,4) and the meeting of the Council where Hastings is denounced (III,4). Nearly 200 lines from Shakespeare's other history plays were inserted and Cibber added over 1,000 lines of his own composition, retained only about 800 lines of Shakespeare's original play, and even made alterations to most of these! It was in Cibber's, not Shakespeare's, version that great actors like David Garrick and Edmund Kean achieved their triumphs. Even today some of the most popular of the sayings of Cibber's Richard ('Off with his head! So much for Buckingham' and 'Richard's himself again') are often mistakenly thought by some people to be Shakespeare's. Samuel Phelps revived Shakespeare's text for a very short time in 1845, but Shakespeare's play was not effectively reinstated until Sir Henry Irving's production of 1877. Even Olivier's film, probably the most popular of all Shakespearian films, incorporates bits of Cibber (as well as lines from *Henry VI, Part 3*).

## Date

Since in Shakespeare's day books had to be licensed, their titles were entered in the register of the Stationers' Company, usually shortly before publication. *Richard III* was registered in 1597 and the first Quarto was published later in the same year. But for various reasons Elizabethan theatre companies did not usually publish their plays until long after their first performances. We do not know how much earlier than 1597 Shakespeare actually wrote *Richard III*. It seems reasonable to assume that it followed the three parts of *Henry VI* and we know that the last of these was acted not later than 1592. Such evidence as we have points to 1592 or 1593 as the date of composition of *Richard III*

# Scene summaries, critical comment, textual notes and revision questions

## Act I Scene 1

The play opens with a soliloquy in which Richard, Duke of Gloucester, explains how his physical deformity prevents him from enjoying the delights of the period of peace which has followed the battle of Tewkesbury. Since he cannot prove a lover, he is 'determined to prove a villain'. He has laid plans to make his brother, King Edward IV, so suspicious of the Duke of Clarence, another brother, that Clarence is to be imprisoned. Richard meets Clarence on his way to prison and pretends to show surprise and sympathy. He insinuates that the responsibility for Clarence's imprisonment lies with Edward's Queen and her own family. As Clarence leaves, Lord Hastings enters, just released from the Tower and determined to get even with those who caused his imprisonment. Left alone, Richard plans to have Clarence murdered and to woo Lady Anne (widow of Prince Edward, who was the son of the dead King Henry VI and who had been killed at Tewkesbury), with a view to gaining the throne for himself. He hopes the King will not live much longer.

## *Commentary*

The scene shows evidence of Shakespeare's early workmanship – for example, the long, explanatory soliloquy at the beginning instead of a more realistic opening. Yet the figure of Richard, with his 'inductions dangerous', is to dominate the play and it is perhaps fitting that he should be presented to us in this way at the very beginning. Notice how much we learn of Richard's character from this scene – his intelligence, his wit, his boldness in action, his hypocrisy, his charm of manner, his singleness of purpose; and how the scene indicates the whole future course of the action – Richard's bid for the throne and his ruthless annihilation of all who oppose him or stand in his way.

**Now** i.e. after the Battle of Tewkesbury and the death of Henry VI in 1471.

**winter of our discontent** This refers to the dreary time during which the house of York had had to endure the rule of the Lancastrians. At the Battle of Tewkesbury the Lancastrian army was utterly defeated,

Prince Edward was slain and Queen Margaret, for many years the real leader of the Lancastrian party, was imprisoned. Shortly afterwards, her husband, Henry VI, was murdered in the Tower.

**son of York** Edward IV, eldest son of the Duke of York, whose revolt at the first battle of St Albans had begun the Wars of the Roses in 1455, now reigned as absolute monarch. Richard's phrase refers particularly to the Yorkist badge, a blazing sun, which had been adopted by Edward partly because it had been the device of Richard II and partly to commemorate the vision of three suns which appeared in the sky before Edward's victory at Mortimer's Cross in 1461.

**bruised arms** Battered weapons.

**monuments** Memorials, reminders.

**alarums** Calls to arms.

**measures** Dances.

**front** Forehead.

**barbed** A barb was a covering made of metal and leather which protected the chest and sides of a horse when it was made ready for battle.

**pleasing** Pleasure. 'He' is 'grim-visag'd War', but in 'lascivious pleasing' and 'amorous looking-glass' there is no doubt an allusion to Edward's amorousness, which is referred to several times later in the play.

**stamp'd** Impressed, shaped. The metaphor is from striking a coin.

**want love's majesty** Lack the dignity of a lover.

**ambling** Walking in an affected way.

**curtail'd . . . proportion** Lacking the handsome physical form necessary for success in such pursuits.

**feature** Comeliness of body.

**dissembling** Deceitful, false.

**Deform'd** The Tudor chroniclers described Richard in terms of monstrous deformity – 'little of stature, ill featured of limbs, crook-backed, his left shoulder much higher than his right, hard-favoured of visage . . . It is for truth reported that he came in the world with feet forward and (as the fame runneth) not untoothed.' There is no contemporary evidence for Richard's deformity.

**breathing world** World of life.

**lamely** Imperfectly.

**unfashionable** Uncouthly. When two adverbs stand closely together in Elizabethan English the adverbial suffix of one of them is often omitted.

**halt** Limp.

**piping time** A time when the pastoral pipe is more suitable than the drums and fifes of war; or perhaps the shrill voices of women and children are contrasted with the martial voices of men.

**descant** Comment. Originally a musical term, meaning to add a part by way of a variation on a simple melody.

**entertain** While away.

**well-spoken days** Days of fair speeches and soft words.

**inductions dangerous** Preparations for mischief.

**mew'd up** Shut up, imprisoned. A mew was originally a cage where falcons were kept while moulting. After 1534, when the royal stables were rebuilt on the site of the royal falcons' cages, the word 'mews' came to mean 'stables'.

**prophecy** The Duke of Clarence's name was George, of course. Holinshed, who mentions the prophecy 'that after K. Edward one should reign whose first letter of his name should be a G', adds that those who believed the prophecy could point out that it actually was fulfilled, since Gloucester as well as George begins with G.

**Tend'ring** Having a tender or high regard for.

**conduct** Escort. Cf. safe-conduct.

**belike** Probably.

**new-christen'd** To Richard's sardonic humour in this speech is added a touch of dramatic irony for an audience who would know the manner of Clarence's death.

**cross-row** Alphabet. In the odd horn-books, or primers, a cross was prefixed to the alphabet, which was often called the criss-cross-row (or Christ's-cross-row).

**for** Because.

**toys** Idle fancies, silly thoughts.

**this it is** This is what happens.

**My Lady Grey** Elizabeth, queen to Edward IV, was born in 1437. She was the daughter of Sir Richard Woodville and married Sir John Grey, who died at the battle of St Albans in 1461. Edward married her in 1464, in spite of his mother's opposition. Elizabeth used her position as Queen to further the interests of her own large family, the Woodvilles, thus arousing the jealousy of the established nobility.

**tempers him to this extremity** Persuades him to take such extreme measures. To temper is to fashion or mould; hence to influence. The Folio reads, 'That tempts him to this harsh extremity.'

**worship** Honour, dignity. Cf. 'Your worship' and 'worshipful' as ceremonial forms of address.

**Anthony Woodeville** Earl Rivers, Lord Scales, and brother to Elizabeth. He was one of the most learned men of his day and a patron of Caxton. In this line 'Woodeville' is pronounced as three syllables.

**Lord Hastings** A faithful supporter of the house of York and much opposed to the relatives of Queen Elizabeth.

**Mistress Shore** Jane Shore was the wife of a London goldsmith and the mistress of Edward IV and later of Hastings. Holinshed says that she had great beauty, 'pleasant behaviour' and 'proper wit', and adds, 'For many that had highly offended she obtained pardon.'

**delivery** Setting at liberty.

**my Lord Chamberlain** i.e. Lord Hastings.

**our way** The best course for us to adopt.

**men** i.e. servants.

**o'er-worn** Faded, the worse for wear. Although Elizabeth was a widow when Edward married her, Richard's adjective is merely contemptuous, for she was only thirty-four at this time.

**dubb'd them gentlewomen**  Again Richard is using words rather loosely, this time to express his contempt for the way these women used their association with the King to gain great influence. Although Elizabeth and her family were already gentlefolk, they were nevertheless exalted by her marriage. Jane Shore was never ennobled, but owing to her influence Richard lumps her with Elizabeth.

**gossips**  Cronies, intimate friends; sometimes, talkative women. The word originally meant a godfather or godmother (from 'godsib', related in God).

**straitly given in charge**  Strictly commanded.

**conference**  Conversation.

**Well struck**  Advanced. In Middle English the verb 'to strike' had the sense of 'to proceed, to move forward'.

**passing**  Surpassingly.

**naught**  Richard puns on 'nought' (nothing) and 'naught' (wickedness). To do naught – to have sexual intercourse.

**withal**  Moreover. This word has several uses in Shakespeare: (1) as an adverb, as here; (2) as an emphatic form of the preposition 'with', generally placed at the end of the sentence, e.g. 'Remember whom you are to cope withal'; and (3) as an adverb meaning 'therewith', e.g. 'And bid her wipe her weeping eyes withal.'

**abjects**  People who are despised or of no account, lit. outcasts. The resemblance of the word to 'subjects' gives Richard's remark a touch of characteristically bitter humour.

**King Edward's widow**  i.e. the widow whom King Edward married.

**enfranchise**  Set at liberty.

**Touches me deeper**  Richard is being deliberately ambiguous. The phrase can mean either 'hurts me more deeply' or 'concerns me more'.

**lie for you**  Again, Richard has in mind the two meanings of the phrase – 'to go to prison for' and 'to tell lies about'.

**new deliver'd**  Lately released.

**Good time of day**  For this general expression we now substitute 'good morning', 'good afternoon', etc as the case may be; but we still use the expression 'to pass the time of day'.

**brook'd**  Endured.

**eagles**  The reference is to Clarence. The 'kites and buzzards' are the Queen's relatives, who are free to strike down their victims at will.

**fear him**  Are anxious about him.

**by Saint John**  Some editions have 'Saint Paul', Richard's favourite oath later in the play, though on this occasion the Folio has 'Saint John'. Sir Thomas More's history makes Richard swear by Saint Paul on one occasion only. 'Perhaps Shakespeare adopted this as Richard's habitual oath, because its Protestant flavour added a touch to the mock-Puritan piety which is one of the more entertaining masks that his Richard assumes' (J. Dover Wilson).

**diet**  Mode of life.

**pack'd with post-horse**  Sent express. Post-horse was the quickest form of travel known at the time, making use of relays of horses stationed at stages of ten miles or so along the highway.

**well-steel'd** Strengthened.

**deep intent** Subtle plan.

**bustle** Bestir myself.

**Warwick's youngest daughter** Warwick, 'the King-maker', had been the chief supporter of the house of York, but when, after the victory of Towton in 1461, Edward became king and it was clear that he intended to rule alone, Warwick gained Clarence (who married Warwick's eldest daughter) on his side and the two joined Margaret and drove Edward into exile. In 1471 Edward returned with a Burgundian army, was rejoined by the vacillating Clarence, and defeated his enemies at Barnet, where Warwick was killed, and at Tewkesbury, where Margaret's son Edward was killed. Warwick's youngest daughter, Anne, had been betrothed to Prince Edward in 1470. They were never actually married, but Shakespeare follows popular tradition in referring to them as man and wife. According to Holinshed, Clarence, Richard, Grey, Dorset and Hastings were all concerned in the death of Prince Edward ('her husband'); but since Richard had no responsibility for the death of Warwick, 'father' is probably used in the sense of father-in-law and refers to Henry VI, whose murder in the Tower was arranged by Richard after the Battle of Tewkesbury. (Shakespeare makes Richard himself kill Henry VI.)

**another secret close intent** Richard believes that Anne's wealth will help him to gain his ultimate end, the crown.

**run before my horse to market** i.e. count my chickens before they are hatched.

## Act I Scene 2

Lady Anne, mourning over the corpse of Henry VI, is met by Richard. She begins by cursing him, but Richard, by his hypocrisy and strength of personality, overcomes her opposition and declares that he killed King Henry and Prince Edward because of his love for her. He flatters her and offers her his life, and finally she accepts his ring. Richard's soliloquy indicates his delight at his success.

### Commentary

This scene has been much criticized because of its improbability. Yet Anne Neville, betrothed to Prince Edward, did in actual fact marry Richard, two years after the Battle of Tewkesbury, in which Edward was killed. But we must note (a) that Shakespeare has drastically telescoped events for dramatic purposes, so that a scene like this was necessary to make it seem even remotely possible that Anne would consent to marry Richard; (b) that Anne does not have the audience's knowledge of Richard's character as revealed in the preceding scene; and (c) that Shakespeare makes great theatrical capital out of the scene by showing us Richard's ability to overcome all opposition by his intelligence and hypocritical charm – the latter being an important feature of his character. Charles Lamb wrote of 'that fine address which was necessary to have betrayed the heart of Lady Anne'. John Palmer notes that Richard's pleasure at his success in wooing Anne springs from his having proved 'that his measureless contempt of human nature, with its weak affections and silly scruples, is justified'. Sir George Macdonald points out that the scene 'increases our admiration for Richard's qualities without making us feel more kindly towards him'.

**hearse**  Bier.

**obsequiously**  As befits a mourner.

**untimely**  Premature.

**Lancaster**  i.e. Henry VI.

**key-cold**  Cold as a key.

**invocate**  Invoke. It was not lawful for Protestants to invoke the Saints. There were attempts to have Henry canonized, and Anne addresses his dead body as though he were actually a Saint. In addition to this speech there are two other passages in the play where Henry is described as 'holy', and in IV,1 Anne refers to him as 'that dead saint'.

**windows**  i.e. his wounds. The metaphor refers to the old custom of opening windows and doors to allow the soul of a dying person to pass out.

**helpless**  Unavailing, without the power to help (*not* 'without help').

**blood . . . blood**  The first 'blood' has the sense of 'anger, passion'. Though to us it may seem a little unnatural, it is not uncommon in Elizabethan literature to find characters indulging in wordplay when under the stress of strong emotion.

**venom'd**  It was popularly believed that both the toad and the spider were poisonous.

**abortive . . . prodigious**  Both words mean 'like a monster'.

**aspect**  Look, appearance.

**unhappiness**  Wickedness, evil nature.

**If ever he have wife . . .**  The play has many such examples of dramatic irony (see note on 'Literary terms', p.15). Dover Wilson points out that 'any wife of such a monster would be happy, not miserable, at his death, while it is not Prince Edward and King Henry who make Anne miserable, but their death'. He refers to Anne's own report of these words in IV,1, and suggests that the two lines here (I,2) should read: 'More miserable by the *life* of him/Than I am by my young lord's death and thee.' ('Thee', addressed to Henry's corpse, implies his death.)

**Chertsey** Holinshed records that Henry VI's body was taken from the
Tower to St Paul's, where it rested for a day, then to Blackfriars, and
thence by boat to the monastery of Chertsey, Surrey, where it was
buried.

**as** As often as.

**devoted charitable deeds** i.e. deeds of devoted charity.

**Advance** Raise.

**Avaunt** Begone.

**minister** Servant, agent.

**curst** Spiteful.

**exclaims** Exclamations, outcries.

**pattern** Example.

**bleed** Holinshed says that Henry VI's corpse was seen to bleed both at
St Paul's and at Blackfriars. Shakespeare combines this legend with the
popular superstition that a murdered man's wounds bleed afresh in
the presence of his murderer.

**exhales** Draws out.

**empty veins** In earlier times it was believed that one effect of death was
to empty the veins of blood.

**Provokes this deluge** An example of hyperbole (see note on 'Literary
terms', p.15), with a biblical reference. Dover Wilson points out that
'monstrous sin had provoked the first deluge', the Flood.

**quick** Alive.

**Lady . . . Villain** The next fifty lines of dialogue are in imitation of the
sticomythia of Greek classical drama (see note on 'Literary terms',
p.15).

**circumstance** Detailed statement, circumstantial evidence.

**diffus'd** Disordered, shapeless. Some editors print 'defus'd'. The
phrase 'diffus'd infection' is more important for its echo of and
contrast with 'divine perfection' than for any real meaning it may
have, though it has an obvious reference to Richard's deformity, of
course.

**Of these known evils . . . self** Many editors follow the Quarto reading
'For . . . curse'. But in her study of *First Folio Textual Problems* Miss
Alice Walker points out that the verbal game which starts with
Richard's 'acquit' in line 77 is carried on with the play on 'accuse' and
'excuse' until line 88. She suggests that these two lines should read: '*Of*
these known evils, but to give me leave/By circumstance, to *accuse* thy
cursed self.

**patient leisure** i.e. patience and leisure.

**current** Accepted as genuine. A metaphor from coinage.

**worthy** Well-deserved.

**falchion** Sword (particularly a broad sword with a curved edge).

**bend** Aim. Originally used of a bow and later applied in this sense to a
sword.

**hedgehog** A term of abuse for a person who pays no regard to the
feelings of others. This could be seen as an allusion to Richard's
hunchback and to his badge, the white boar, or hog.

**holp**  Some editions have 'help'd', but 'holp' is the usual form of the past tense in Shakespeare.

**timeless**  Untimely.

**effect**  Agent. In the next line the word has its usual meaning.

**to be reveng'd on thee**  She means that she would then be able to make him miserable.

**Plantagenet**  Richard himself and the dead Prince Edward were both Plantagenets.

**infect**  Pollute.

**infected**  i.e. with love-sickness.

**basilisks**  A basilisk was a fabulous reptile, believed to have the power of killing by its look. It was supposed to be hatched by a serpent from a cock's egg and was sometimes called a cockatrice.

**at once**  Once and for all.

**living death**  A life that resembles death. An example of oxymoron (see note on 'Literary terms', p.15).

**Sham'd their aspects**  Disgraced their appearance.

**remorseful**  Full of pity.

**Rutland**  Richard's brother, the second son of Richard, Duke of York. He was murdered after the Battle of Wakefield, in 1460.

**thy warlike father**  See note on 'Warwick's youngest daughter', p.26. In Shakespeare's *Henry VI, Part 3* the 'sad story' is told by a messenger, not by Warwick.

**my father's death**  When Richard, Duke of York, was captured at the Battle of Wakefield, Queen Margaret showed him a napkin stained with the blood of his son, Rutland, and mocked him by placing a paper crown upon his head. He was then stabbed to death by Clifford and Queen Margaret.

**Like trees . . . rain**  Richard's speeches sometimes have effective poetical touches like this. But how sincere are they?

**smoothing**  Flattering.

**the death**  One is reminded of the phrase of judicial sentence, 'to die the death'.

**dissembler**  Hypocrite.

**for thy love . . . a far truer lover**  In both these lines the second 'love' means 'lover', in the first line referring to Prince Edward, in the second to Richard himself.

**figur'd**  Represented.

**your sword**  Her use of 'your' for the first time seems to mark the moment when Anne finally relents; up to this point she has used 'thou' and 'thy' by way of contempt. In Elizabethan times speakers generally continued the Middle English practice of using 'you' and 'your' in addressing superiors and equals, and reserving 'thou' and 'thy' for inferiors.

**To take . . . to give**  'Although I accept your ring, I give you no pledge of troth in return' (Macdonald).

**sad designs**  i.e. your intention to mourn for Henry VI.

**presently**  Immediately.

**Crosby Place** Richard's house in Bishopsgate Street. It was built by Sir
  John Crosby. Part of it still survives as Crosby Hall.
**expedient duty** Swift respect.
**unknown** Secret.
**With all my heart** It seems that Anne's assent is quite sincere and
  genuine, for in IV,1 she says that her woman's heart 'grew captive to
  his honey words' – though by that time she realizes her folly.
**'Tis more** i.e. to fare well is more.
**Whitefriars** A Carmelite priory which stood on the south side of Fleet
  Street.
**three months** There was actually less than three weeks between the
  Battle of Tewkesbury and the burial of Henry's body. Shakespeare
  extends the interval to make Anne's acceptance of Richard appear less
  improbable.
**prodigality of Nature** i.e. when Nature was in a generous mood; she
  bestowed upon him so many qualities.
**moiety** This word, which originally meant a half, came to be used for
  any small part, as here.
**denier** 'A denier is the twelfth part of a French sou, and seems to have
  been the regular request of a beggar' (Steevens).
**proper** Handsome.
**be at charges for** Bear the expense of.
**entertain** Engage, employ.


## Act I Scene 3

Richard boldly defies the Queen and her relatives, charging
them with being responsible for the imprisonment of Hastings
and Clarence. During the ensuing quarrel Queen Margaret,
widow of King Henry VI, appears. At first she remains in the
background, uttering her hatred of Richard in 'asides'; later she
comes forward and lays her curses on King Edward, Prince
Edward (his son), Queen Elizabeth, Rivers, Dorset, Hastings,
and finally Richard. She warns Buckingham to beware of
Richard. The scene closes with Richard's ordering two murderers to kill Clarence swiftly.


## *Commentary*

The entrance of Queen Margaret introduces an important
motive in the play – the theme of Nemesis. She prophesies that
vengeance shall fall not only on Richard but on the whole house
of York for the wrongs done to the house of Lancaster. In the
course of the play each victim at his death recalls her curses.
Although he does not realize it, Richard himself is the instru-

ment of vengeance, and when Margaret appears in IV,4 she exults in the fulfilment of her prophecies.

**brook** See note p.25.

**entertain** Receive, take.

**quick** Lively.

**betide on** Happen to.

**nor none** In Shakespeare double negatives give added emphasis.

**determin'd, not concluded** Settled, though not yet formally decreed. One chronicler (Polydore Vergil) says that when Edward made his will 'he constituted his sons his heirs, whom he committed to the tuition of Richard his brother, Duke of Gloucester'. Richard was first made Protector at a meeting of the Council after Edward V's arrival in London from Ludlow.

**miscarry** Die.

**Countess Richmond** Margaret Beaufort, great-granddaughter of John of Gaunt, married Edmund Tudor, Earl of Richmond. (The latter was the son of Owen Tudor and Henry V's widow, Katharine.) Their son was the Richmond of this play, who became Henry VII, the first of the Tudor kings. Margaret Beaufort's third husband was Lord Stanley, a widower with three sons, the eldest of whom was 'young George Stanley' (see V,5).

**arrogance** i.e. in aspiring to the crown for her son.

**envious** Malicious.

**wayward sickness** Weakness that makes people perverse.

**amendment** Recovery.

**atonement** Reconciliation (lit. 'at-one-ment', being 'at one' with others).

**brothers** Earl Rivers was the Queen's only brother (see note on 'Anthony Woodeville', p.24). Shakespeare wrongly takes her son Grey to be her brother.

**warn** Call.

**They do me wrong** Notice the effectiveness of Richard's sudden entry with a speech which immediately carries the attack into the enemy camp and which shows that the King's attempt at reconciliation will be unsuccessful. It is one of Richard's great qualities that in any situation he always takes the initiative. Notice too his subtlety in claiming to be a 'plain man' full of 'simple truth'. As Macdonald points out, this openness is only a more dangerous form of hypocrisy.

**dissentious** Seditious.

**smooth** Flatter.

**cog** Cheat.

**French nods** Foreign manners were often, and still are, ridiculed by English writers.

**silken** Effeminate.

**Jacks** Low, common fellows.

**in all this presence** Among all the persons here present.

**Cannot . . . scarce** Can hardly

**breathing while**  A very short time.

**lewd**  Vile, base.

**The king . . . to send**  The construction of the sentence is confused (perhaps in order to represent the Queen's incoherence in the presence of a dangerous enemy), but the meaning is clear: 'The king sends for you, not because he has been incited to do so by anyone else, but of his own free will, because he sees that your actions towards my family show that you possess an inner hatred of us.'

**gentle**  Of gentle birth.

**that we have need of you**  i.e. that I (Richard) am in distress owing to you (Elizabeth). Richard is making a play on the double sense of 'need'.

**noble**  A coin of little value. Note the pun.

**careful**  Full of care.

**injury**  Injustice.

**draw . . . suspects**  Involve me in these vile suspicions.

**marry**  On the first two occasions the word is used as an exclamation (from the name of the Virgin Mary); on the third it is a verb with its usual sense.

**Iwis**  Certainly. Cf. German *gewiss*.

**condition**  Stipulation.

**due to me**  My due, mine by right.

**adventure to be**  Take the risk of being.

**my pains**  i.e. the trouble I took to gain the throne for Edward.

**pack-horse**  Drudge, lit. horse of burden.

**Grey**  Sir John Grey was a Lancastrian, but in *Henry VI, Part 3* Shakespeare mistakenly says he fell fighting for the Yorkists.

**factious for**  On the side of.

**battle**  Army.

**Withal**  Moreover. See note p.25.

**father**  i.e. father-in-law. See note on 'Warwick's youngest daughter', p.26.

**party**  Side.

**meed**  Reward. Notice the word-play with 'mew'd up' (see note p.24).

**childish-foolish**  Childishly simple.

**cacodemon**  Evil spirit.

**pill'd**  Robbed, plundered.

**Which of you . . . rebels**  When you look at me you all tremble, if not as subjects bowing before your queen, then at least as quaking rebels before a queen whom you have deposed.

**gentle villain**  Following Dr Johnson, Dover Wilson points out that this is 'a kind of double oxymoron, since "gentle" = (a) well-born, (b) kindly, and "villain" = (a) peasant, (b) scoundrel'.

**what mak'st thou?**  What are you doing?

**But . . . marr'd**  I merely make a recital of your crimes. Notice the proverbial antithesis between 'make' and 'mar'.

**banished**  Not historical fact. After the Battle of Tewkesbury Margaret was a prisoner until 1475, when she was ransomed and returned to

France. She died there in 1482, a year before the death of Edward IV. Her appearance in Shakespeare's play is quite unhistorical.

**abode**  Act of abiding.

**thou**  The first 'thou' is addressed to Richard, the second to Queen Elizabeth.

**When thou didst crown**  The events referred to here took place after the Battle of Wakefield in 1460. See note on 'my father's death', p.29.

**clout**  Piece of cloth.

**faultless**  Innocent.

**plagu'd**  Punished.

**that babe**  Rutland was in fact in his teens at the time of his death. For dramatic purposes Shakespeare made him a young child.

**Should all but answer for**  Could all not quite pay for.

**peevish**  Silly.

**quick**  Animated.

**surfeit**  Excessive indulgence.

**stall'd**  Installed.

**But by**  i.e. but that you may be by.

**unlook'd**  Unexpected.

**them**  i.e. Heaven, the powers that be.

**still**  Constantly, always.

**elvish-mark'd**  Disfigured at birth by malignant fairies.

**abortive**  See note p.27.

**rooting**  Digging up with its snout. A contemptuous reference to Richard's badge, a white boar.

**seal'd . . . Nature**  Refers to the practice of masters branding their most vicious slaves. By branding him at birth with deformity Nature has made Richard the most degenerate of her slaves.

**rag**  i.e. worthless fragment. Cf. our phase, 'rag-tag and bob-tail'.

**Margaret!**  Richard interrupts her curse by substituting her own name for his. Margaret's 'Richard!' is intended to finish her speech and name the subject of her curse. By then saying 'Ha!' (equivalent to the modern 'Eh?' or 'What do you say?'), he pretends that *he* had already completed her curse for her and that she now calls him. When she denies this, he pretends to understand her reply in a different sense ('I did not call you *these names*'). This is a characteristic example of Richard's quick wit. The reader will better understand the exchange, and the business of 'Ha!' and 'call', if he realizes that during the curse Richard will have turned his back upon Margaret and walked away.

**cry thee mercy**  Beg your pardon.

**period**  Conclusion.

**painted**  Sham, unreal, pretended.

**vain flourish**  Empty show, lit. worthless embellishment.

**bottled**  Shaped like a leather bottle, hence hump-backed.

**bunch-back'd**  Hump-backed. See note on 'venom'd, p.27.

**false-boding**  Prophesying false things.

**well serv'd**  Treated according to your deserts. Margaret plays upon the phrase in her reply. She also turns the meaning of 'duty'. Rivers meant, 'What you should do, how you should behave'; Margaret's 'do me duty' means 'make obeisance to me'. In the last line of her speech 'duty' means 'respect, reverence'. Such complex playing with words is characteristic of Shakespeare's early plays.

**malapert** Impudent.

**fire-new** Brand-new, lit. of a coin ('stamp') fresh from the mint and not yet in general circulation. Sir Thomas Grey, Elizabeth's eldest son by her first husband, had been made Marquess of Dorset only eight years earlier.

**They that stand . . . pieces** Remember that these were the days when high position often depended on the king's favour, which might be short-lived.

**aery** Brood of young eagles (i.e. the house of York).

**dallies** Trifles. Richard means that his rank is so high that there is no danger of a fall.

**Uncharitably . . . butcher'd** Since Margaret in her next speech exempts Buckingham from her charges, some editors have questioned whether the previous speech ('Peace, peace! . . .') should be given to Buckingham. But on the stage there is no problem: Margaret addresses only one line ('Urge neither charity . . .') to Buckingham, before turning to Richard.

**my hopes** i.e. her husband and her son.

**My charity . . . shame** The play on words makes the sense obscure. The meaning seems to be: Instead of charity I have received injustice, and my shame comes not from death but from continuing to live after all that my family has suffered. Note the further play on 'outrage' and 'rage'.

**I will not . . . ascend** I cannot believe that they do not ascend.

**rankle** Fester.

**soothe** Flatter.

**muse** Wonder.

**vantage** Benefit.

**hot** Eager.

**somebody** i.e. Edward IV.

**frank'd up to fatting** Shut up in a sty (frank) to be fattened for slaughter.

**scath(e)** Harm, injury. (Different editions have different spellings.)

**well-advis'd** Careful how I act.

**set abroach** Let loose, lit. to tap a barrel of liquor by piercing it with a spike (broach).

**gulls** Simpletons.

**Dorset** Some editions, following the Quartos, have 'Vaughan' (always pronounced as two syllables in this play). Sir Thomas Vaughan was an attendant on the Prince of Wales.

**sudden** Swift.

**well-spoken** Eloquent.

**millstones** It seems to have been a proverbial expression that hard-hearted people wept millstones.

## Act I Scene 4

In the Tower Clarence recounts a dream in which he thought he was drowned and was greeted in the underworld by Warwick, who accused him of treachery, and by Prince Edward, who charged him with his death at Tewkesbury. The two murderers appear. The Second Murderer is troubled by his conscience, but the First Murderer kills Clarence.

### Commentary

Notice how the difference in the characters of the murderers is brought out and how the horror and tension of the scene are relieved by their humorous dialogue and by our knowledge of Clarence's treachery. Yet the Second Murderer's final repentance emphasizes Richard's unnatural cruelty in ordering the murder of his own brother.

**Christian faithful**  Full of Christian faith.

**Methought(s)**  It seemed to me.

**Burgundy**  i.e. the Low Countries, then under Burgundian rule. Margaret, the sister of Edward, Clarence and Richard, had married the Duke of Burgundy in 1468, and during the Wars of the Roses the Yorkists had often sought refuge in the Burgundian dominions.

**hatches**  Deck.

**cited up**  Recalled.

**unvalu'd**  Invaluable.

**envious**  Malignant.

**bulk**  Body. It has no connection with the commoner word meaning 'size'.

**I pass'd**  Some editions, following the Folio, read 'Who pass'd'. The antecedent for the relative pronoun is understood as being contained in 'my' in the previous line.

**melancholy flood**  The Styx, one of the rivers of the underworld in Greek mythology.

**sour ferryman**  Charon, who ferried the spirits of the dead across the Styx.

**perjury**  See note on 'Warwick's youngest daughter', p.26.

**shadow**  Shade, departed spirit. This is Prince Edward.

**shriek'd**  Some editions read 'squeak'd'. In Shakespeare's day it was a stage tradition that ghosts spoke in a high, shrill voice (in *Hamlet* they 'squeak and gibber', and in *Julius Caesar* they 'shriek and squeal').

**fleeting**  Fickle, inconstant.

**Furies**  Avenging goddesses of Greek mythology.

**wife**  Clarence's wife, Isabella Neville, eldest daughter of Warwick, had actually died some time before. By imagining that she was still alive

Shakespeare heightens the pathos of Clarence's death.

**for their glories**  As their glories.

**for an inward toil**  In return for their inner turmoil.

**for unfelt imaginations**  Instead of happiness, which they imagine they will possess but which they never feel.

**brief**  Dispensing with ceremony and courtesy.

**reason**  Discuss.

**will be . . . meaning**  Wish to be ignorant of the purpose.

**passionate**  Compassionate. Some editions, following the Quartos, have 'holy humour' (i.e. pious feeling).

**tells**  Counts.

**entertain**  Receive. See note p.31.

**checks**  Reproves.

**blushing**  Causing one to blush.

**shamefaced**  Bashful. Some editions read 'shamefast'. The latter is the correct form of the word. It has no connection with 'face' but means 'fixed (fast) in modesty (shame)'.

**Take . . . mind.**  Either (1) choose the devil (the evil purpose) which is in your mind, rather than your conscience which is at your elbow; or (2) arrest that devil of a conscience which lurks in your mind.

**tall**  Brave.

**fall to work**  Some editions, following the Quartos, have 'to this gear' (i.e. this business).

**take**  Strike.

**costard**  Head (a slang term, lit. a large apple).

**throw**  Some editions, following the Quartos, read 'chop' (i.e. thrust, pop).

**malmsey-butt**  Cask of malmsey wine. Malmsey is a strong, sweet wine from Greece.

**sop**  A piece of bread or cake put into a cup of wine.

**reason**  Talk.

**Where art thou, keeper?**  After the awakening of Clarence the dialogue returns to blank verse to mark the heightened feeling of the rest of the scene.

**Where is the evidence**  Some editions read 'Where are the evidence' (i.e. body of witnesses).

**quest**  Jury. Shakespeare ignores the fact that Clarence was actually tried by his peers and found guilty of a whole series of crimes against the King.

**Erroneous**  Misled, or perhaps wicked.

**dear**  Dire, grievous.

**gallant-springing**  Growing up with manly promise.

**novice**  Youth, lit. newly made knight.

**My brother's love**  i.e. love for my brother.

**Thy brother's love**  This involves a play on words – the love we bear thy brother (which is how Clarence understands it), and the love of thy brother for thee (which is how the murderer understands it).
Moreover, the murderer speaks of Richard, but Clarence is thinking of Edward.

**Ay, so we will**  But they will go for a very different purpose from that which Clarence supposes – to report to Richard the accomplishment of their deed.

**lesson'd**  Instructed.

**kind**  Affectionate. The murderer interprets the word in the sense of 'natural'; hence his sarcastic reply.

**labour**  Work for, try to bring about.

**if thine eye . . .**  Unless you are more hardened than your looks suggest.

**give order**  Some editions read 'take order', i.e. make arrangements.

## Revision questions on Act I

**1** Write a brief account of the historical situation when the play opens.

**2** The second scene of the play has been criticized on the grounds of improbability. What are your views? Give full reasons.

**3** Are you entirely sympathetic towards Lady Anne? Do you detect any weaknesses in her character?

**4** What is the dramatic function of Queen Margaret in Scene 3?

**5** By means of a careful analysis of the speeches of the two murderers, show how Shakespeare clearly distinguishes their characters.

**6** How far did Clarence deserve to die?

**7** What examples can you find in Act I of Richard's subtle use of words?

## Act II Scene 1

The sick King Edward attempts to bring about a reconciliation of the quarrelling nobles. Richard enters, professes peace and friendship with all present, and immediately charges the Queen and her relatives with being responsible for Clarence's death. Lord Stanley's plea for the life of his servant is a contrast to the King's remorse for the death of Clarence.

### *Commentary*

The many religious terms used by Edward and the amity he establishes between the factious nobles and the Queen, in dialogue liberally dressed in words like 'love', 'unity' and 'duty', are dramatically contrasted with Richard's hypocritical delight in his display of mock piety and his use of Clarence's death to destroy Edward's 'blessed labour' of reconciliation. A further contrast is provided by Edward's final moving speech and what we have already heard from Richard (I,1) of his 'evil diet' of licentious living.

**embassage** Message.
**part** Depart.
**Dissemble not your hatred** i.e. do not disguise your hatred under a look of friendship.
**dally** Trifle.
**Confound** Bring to nought.
**award** Decree.
**have been factious** Have taken sides in a quarrel.
**but . . . Doth cherish** And does not cherish. Note the dramatic irony of this speech, in view of Richard's subsequent treatment of Buckingham.
**period** Completion. Some editions read 'perfect' instead of 'blessed'.
**in good time** Opportunely.
**swelling** i.e. with anger.
**wrong-incensed** Perversely enraged, or perhaps enraged because they believe they have suffered wrong.
**heap** Great company.
**intelligence** Information.
**hardly borne** Resented.
**humility** Some editors gloss this as 'humanity'.
**compounded** Settled.
**Mercury** The messenger of the gods in classical mythology. He wore winged sandals and a winged hat.
**lag** Late.
**blood** Kinship. Richard is hinting at the Queen's upstart relatives.
**current** Accepted as genuine.
**from** Free from.
**the forfeit . . . life** i.e. I beg my servant's life, which he should legally forfeit.
**was thought** i.e. never put into action.
**When Oxford** This incident is invented by Shakespeare.
**lap** Wrap.
**thin** i.e. thinly covered.
**waiting vassals** Serving-men.
**image** i.e. man, whom God created 'in His own image'.
**beholding** Indebted.
**I fear Thy justice** The last words we hear from Edward are of remorse and impending nemesis. In this way Shakespeare makes the audience feel that Edward's death, like that of Clarence, was deserved.
**help me** One of the duties of Hastings as Lord Chamberlain.
**This** i.e. this outburst of remorse.

## Act II Scene 2

The Duchess of York unsuccessfully attempts to hide from Clarence's two children the death of their father. The Queen announces the death of King Edward, and all four characters join in a chorus of lamentation. Richard and Buckingham make plans to bring the new king, Edward V, from Ludlow to London, with a small escort.

### Commentary

The play is notable for the number of children among the characters and the amount of dialogue which Shakespeare provides for them. Here, and in II,4 and III,1, they contribute much to the pathos in the play.

**cousins** This word was used loosely in Elizabethan English to refer to any collateral relative, just as today one might call a boy 'son' or 'sonny', without any suggestion of the actual relationship. Here it means 'grandchildren', and in III,1 'nephew'. When Richard addresses Buckingham as 'cousin' he uses it in its modern sense – the two men were second cousins.

**God will revenge it** An exact echo of Richard's words at the end of the previous scene. The word 'revenge' tolls like a bell throughout the play.

**Incapable** Unable to understand.

**impeachments** Accusations.

**virtuous vizor** Semblance of virtue. Some editions read 'vizard' (another form of 'vizor').

**brief** Speedy.

**interest . . . title** Legal metaphors. The words mean 'concern' and 'right' respectively.

**images** i.e. children. The 'two mirrors' are Edward and Clarence, the 'false glass' is Richard.

**moiety** See note p.30.

**overgo** Exceed.

**complaints** Lamentations (utterances of grief, not utterances of a grievance.)

**All springs reduce** May all springs bring. In this hyperbole or 'conceit' (see note on 'Literary terms', p.15) the Queen desires that her eyes should be like the ocean, which may receive water from all the rivers so that, through the tidal influence of the moon, it may deluge the world.

**parcell'd** i.e. they have their own particular woes, I have the woes of all. 'Parcel' originally meant 'portion' (cf. our phrase 'part and parcel').

**opposite with** Antagonistic towards.

**requires** Demands the return of.

**Enter Richard**  Shakespeare invents Richard's part in this scene; at the time of Edward's death he was in the north of England. Rivers was at Ludlow.

**butt-end**  Extreme end.

**cloudy**  Gloomy, melancholy.

**mutual**  Common, weighing on all alike.

**moan**  Grief.

**preserv'd**  It is, of course, not the 'rancour' which must be preserved but the concord implied by the whole of the two previous lines.

**train**  Escort.

**Ludlow**  The Prince of Wales, with Lord Rivers, had been sent by Edward IV to Ludlow Castle, formerly a royal residence, in Shropshire, to maintain order among the Welsh.

**lest . . . break out**  The real reason was that Rivers might be more easily seized. Richard seems quite content to let Buckingham take the intiative here.

**estate**  State, kingdom.

**bears . . . rein**  Controls its own guiding-rein.

**apparent likelihood**  Obvious possibility.

**much company**  Large escort.

**censures**  Opinions.

**sort occasion**  Contrive an opportunity.

**index**  Introduction.

**consistory**  Council-chamber, here used to mean secret fount of wisdom. The elaborate flattery makes it clear that Richard is using Buckingham as a cat's paw, while making him believe that he is the initiator of action.


## Act II Scene 3

Three citizens discuss the chances of peaceful government now that King Edward is dead.


### Commentary

The scene allows time for the coup of Richard and Buckingham and the arrest of Rivers and Grey. It foreshadows the struggle for the throne which is now beginning and provides a background for this struggle by showing us the lives of ordinary citizens, who are shrewd enough to realize the true motives of the nobles.

Notice how, even in such a short scene, Shakespeare does much to distinguish the characters of the three citizens.

**giddy**  Uncertain, changing with bewildering rapidity.

**hold**  Hold good, remain true

**the while**  The present time.
**Woe . . . child**  See Ecclesiastes, 10, 16.
**in his nonage**  As long as he is under age. The language of this sentence
  is compressed, but the meaning is clear – we can hope for good
  government from his council during his minority and from himself
  when he takes over control.
**wot**  Knows.
**emulation**  Rivalry.
**touch . . . near**  Seriously afflict.
**haught**  Haughty.
**solace**  Find comfort.
**sort**  Dispose, ordain. Cf. note p.40.
**cannot . . . almost**  Can hardly.
**mistrust Ensuing danger**  Anticipate approaching catastrophe.
**proof**  Experience.

## Act II Scene 4

Members of the house of York await the arrival of the young
King, but they learn that Richard has struck his first blow by
arresting Rivers, Grey and Vaughan. Queen Elizabeth foresees
the downfall of the house of York, and the Duchess recalls the
vicissitudes of the family in their long struggle for the crown.
They take refuge from danger by going to the sanctuary of
Westminster, taking with them the young Duke of York.

### *Commentary*

The words of the Duchess and the young Duke of York under-
line the growing dislike of Richard.

**Stony-Stratford**  A market town in Buckinghamshire.
**gracious**  Virtuous, godly.
**had been remember'd**  Had remembered.
**my uncle's Grace**  A play of words – 'the virtue of my uncle' and 'His
  Grace, my uncle'.
**flout**  Gibe.
**touch**  Strike at.
**they say**  York's 'biting jest' refers to the popular rumour that Richard
  was born with all his teeth.
**parlous**  Mischievous. A corruption of 'perilous'.
**Pitchers**  Cf. the proverb, 'Little pitchers have wide ears' – children
  often overhear things they should not.
**Pomfret**  Pontefract Castle, in West Yorkshire, where Richard II was
  imprisoned.
**can**  Know.
**Insulting**  Scornfully triumphant.

**jut** Encroach. Some editions read 'jet', another form of the same word.

**map** A picture representing much detail in a condensed form. This type of picture (and this use of the word) was common in Shakespeare's day.

**Clean over-blown** Completely passed away (like a storm). The Duchess's speech is one of the many reminders in this play of recent bloody events.

**blood to blood** Kinsman against kinsman.

**preposterous** Contrary to nature (lit. back to front).

**spleen** Malice.

**earth** Some editions, following the Quartos, read 'death'.

**sanctuary** By the law of the medieval Church, a fugitive from justice or a debtor was immune from arrest in a church or other sacred place. Here the sanctuary of Westminster Abbey is meant.

**seal** i.e. The Great Seal, the emblem and instrument of sovereignty, of which the Archbishop was the keeper.

**tender** See note on 'tend'ring', p.24.


## Revision questions on Act II

1 Why does Shakespeare introduce Lord Stanley's plea for his servant in Scene 1?

2 What examples do you find of formal language and repetition in Scene 2?

3 Outline the part played by Buckingham in Acts I and II.

4 What is the dramatic purpose of Act II, Scene 3?

5 By means of a detailed analysis of the speeches of the three citizens, show how Shakespeare distinguishes their characters.


## Act III Scene 1

The young King is welcomed into London by Richard, Buckingham and the Lord Mayor. Hastings and the Archbishop of Canterbury are sent to bring the Duke of York from sanctuary, and Richard suggests that the King shall be lodged in the Tower. After the King has joined his brother there follows a conversation with Richard which is dark with irony, before the two brothers are taken to the Tower. Catesby is sent to sound Hastings and to find out his reaction to the plan formed by Buckingham and Richard to make the latter king. Richard says that when he is king Buckingham may claim from him the earldom of Hereford.

## *Commentary*

Notice the differences between the characters of the two Princes. The young King is thoughtful and melancholy – it is not only that he is conscious of his new responsibility; it is as if imminent events are casting their shadow before. The Duke of York is 'bold, quick, ingenious, forward, capable'. His precocious remarks, with Richard's replies and his grim 'asides', make this scene full of tragic irony.

**chamber** Royal residence. London was known as *camera regis,* the king's chamber.

**crosses** Troubles, i.e. the arrest of his uncle Rivers and others of his mother's relatives.

**jumpeth** Agrees with.

**slug** Sluggard.

**Anon** At once, lit. in one.

**senseless-obstinate** Foolishly obstinate.

**ceremonious and traditional** Scrupulous about forms and observant of customs.

**Weigh . . . age** i.e. consider the matter broadly, by the standards of the present day.

**wit** Understanding.

**I do not . . . any place** i.e. I like the Tower least of all places.

**Julius Caesar** It was a popular tradition that Julius Caesar built the Tower of London. It was actually begun in the reign of William the Conqueror.

**re-edified** Rebuilt, repaired.

**retail'd** Reported, related.

**without characters** Even without written records.

**formal Vice, Iniquity** The conventional figure of Vice in the old morality plays, a comic buffoon.

**moralize** Explain, comment upon. Richard means that he has two explanations of 'live long', the only part of his previous 'aside' that the Prince might have heard.

**And if** For 'And' some editions read 'An', which itself means 'if'; but the use of the double conjunction was very common.

**lightly** Commonly, often.

**cousin** See note p.39.

**idle** Useless.

**My dagger . . . heart** Notice the double meaning – Richard is soon to plan the deaths of the princes.

**toy** Trifle.

**light** Notice the play upon the two meanings of the word – light in weight and light in value.

**I weigh . . . heavier** I would consider it a trifle even it if were heavier.

**He thinks . . . shoulders** This is a gibe at Richard's hunchback and perhaps refers to the saddle in which the strolling buffoon carried his monkey. Dover Wilson quotes from *Plaine Percevall* (about 1590): 'You are thinking belike to ride upon my croup shoulders [i.e. hunchback]: I am no Ape Carrier.' Dr Johnson has another interpretation: 'The reproach seems to consist in this: at country shows it was common to set the monkey on the back of some other animal, as a bear. The Duke, therefore, in calling himself an *ape* calls his uncle a *bear*.'

**sharp-provided** Keen and ready.

**if they live** He is thinking of his uncle Rivers.

*Sennet* A set of notes played on a trumpet at the approach or departure of a procession.

**parlous** See note p.41.

**capable** Intelligent.

**Come hither, Catesby** Once again it pleases Richard to let Buckingham play the leader.

**doth stand affected** Is disposed.

**sit** Attend a meeting of the council.

**divided councils** The chroniclers explain how Richard summoned two councils. His accomplices met at Crosby Place to give him the crown, while the supporters of Edward V met at the Tower to make arrangements for the latter's coronation.

**ancient knot** Old gang. Since 'knot' could mean 'tumour' as well as 'an evil company', there may be a pun with 'let blood', i.e. surgically bled – a euphemism for 'killed'.

**Mistress Shore** See note p.24.

**complots** Conspiracies.

**moveables** Personal property (as distinct from lands and houses).

**digest** Arrange.

## Act III Scene 2

The over-confident Hastings refuses to listen to a warning message from Lord Stanley. After being sounded by Catesby, Hastings refuses to support Richard's bid for the throne. He rejoices in the news that Rivers, Grey and Vaughan are to die and says he will shortly arrange the deaths of other enemies of his. When Stanley arrives, Hastings mocks at his fears.

### *Commentary*

This scene is full of lines which are packed with irony. Catesby, Buckingham and the audience know that Richard has decided to execute Hastings if the latter does not fall in with his plans; but Hastings is unaware of the significance of many of their remarks and of the 'dramatic irony' which lies in many of the expressions of his own self-assurance. Notice how his emptiness, his cruelty

and his intolerable self-confidence mean that later the audience
will be prepared to accept his death without any compassion.

**certifies** Assures.

**boar** i.e. Richard.

**razed** Plucked, pulled.

**his** i.e. Stanley's

**without instance** Groundless. Some editions read 'wanting instance'.
The meaning is the same.

**simple** Some editions read 'fond' i.e. foolish.

**kindly** Hastings means 'gently', but Shakespeare's audience would also
be aware of the word's other meaning at that time, 'after his nature',
i.e. cruelly.

**this crown of mine** Shakespeare often makes use of this pun.

**foul** Wrongfully.

**to the death** At the risk of my life.

**The princes both** Applied to Buckingham, 'prince' is a form of
compliment, even though Buckingham was the next heir to the throne
after Richard.

**they account . . . Bridge** They reckon on having his head set up on
London Bridge, where traitors' heads were stuck upon poles and
exposed to public view.

**Rood** Cross.

**several** Separate.

**but that I** If I did not.

**state** Position.

**mistrust** Expect danger.

**misdoubt** Have misgivings about.

**have with you** Come along.

**for their truth** In respect of their loyalty.

**wear their hats** This has been explained as 'keep their offices'.

*Pursuivant* The attendant of a herald.

**suggestion** Instigation.

**hold** Continue.

**Gramercy** A form of words to acknowledge an inferior's good wishes.
From Old Fr. *grant merci*, '(God give you) great reward'.

**Sir John** 'Sir' was a common form of address to an ordained
clergyman.

**exercise** Sermon or act of worship.

**content** Satisfy, i.e. pay.

**no shriving work** No need for confession and absolution.

**supper** i.e. the last meal of the day. It will be Hastings's last meal on
earth.

## Act III Scene 3

At Pomfret Castle, Rivers, Grey and Vaughan go to their deaths remembering the curses which Margaret laid upon them.

### Commentary

This short scene strikingly links the past and the future: on the one hand the reference to the tragic death of Richard II and the emphasis on Margaret's curse, on the other the prophetic words of Vaughan (line 6) and Rivers (lines 17–19), calling for a heavenly justice which will eventually catch up with Richard himself.

**truth**  Faithfulness.
**knot**  See note on 'ancient knot' p.44.
**limit**  Prescribed time.
**ominous**  Among the 'noble peers' who died or were killed at Pontefract Castle were Thomas, Earl of Lancaster (1322), Archbishop Scrope (1405) and Salisbury (1461). Richard II died here in 1399.
**closure**  Enclosure.
**slander to**  Disgrace to.
**expiate**  Fully come.

## Act III Scene 4

At a meeting of the Council to make arrangements for the coronation of the young King, Hastings is full of confidence and presumes to speak for Richard. When Richard appears he accuses Queen Elizabeth and Jane Shore of practising witchcraft upon him and charges Hastings, as protector of Jane Shore, with treason, ordering his immediate execution. Hastings too now recalls Margaret's curse.

### Commentary

Richard's initial affability, the presumption of Hastings and the cautious duplicity of Buckingham are all skilfully presented through dialogue which places much emphasis on the difference between appearance and reality, between 'faces' and 'hearts', and prepares us for Richard's sudden change of mood and the consequent reversal of Hastings's fortunes.

**wants but nomination**  All that is wanting is the fixing of the day.

**inward**  Intimate.

**knows no more of mine**  Buckingham does not realize how well Richard understands him!

**in the Duke's behalf**  The Lord Chamberlain frequently served as the royal mouthpiece in the Council. Nevertheless, we are meant to regard Hastings's action as presumptuous.

**sleeper**  Actually Richard had been at the secret council at Crosby Place.

**neglect**  Cause to be neglected.

**upon your cue**  At the very moment when you were required to speak. A cue is a word or phrase at the end of a speech which serves as a signal to another actor to begin. The theatrical metaphor is continued in 'part'.

**voice**  Vote or expression of opinion.

**Holborn**  Ely Palace stood in Holborn, in what is now called Hatton Garden. Shakespeare took the incident of the strawberries from Holinshed, who had it from Sir Thomas More's *History*. More's patron, Cardinal Morton, was the Bishop of Ely of this scene and one of the principal instruments of Richard's downfall. The incident is not important to the plot but it shows how Richard hides his duplicity behind a facade of geniality, gives him an excuse for not discussing the coronation and perhaps an opportunity to withdraw with Buckingham, and provides a dramatic contrast to his re-entrance a few moments later.

**triumph**  Public festivity or ceremonial.

**prolong'd**  Postponed.

**conceit**  Ingenious idea. Hastings would be surprised if he knew what it was!

**livelihood**  Most editors read 'likelihood', outward sign.

**I pray you all**  Holinshed says: 'He returned to the chamber . . . with a wonderful sour angry countenance, knitting the brows, frowning and fretting, and gnawing on his lips.'

**doom**  Judge.

**consorted with**  In league with. Dover Wilson points out that Jane Shore is dragged in so as to catch Hastings, who falls into the trap. After the death of Edward IV, Jane Shore had become Hastings's mistress.

**Ratcliffe**  It has been suggested that Shakespeare meant this to be Catesby, since Ratcliffe was at Pontefract (see the previous scene), and that the confusion arose because one actor may have taken both parts. Certainly there is little to distinguish Richard's three henchmen, Catesby, Ratcliffe and Lovell, who figure in a famous satire of Richard's day which begins: 'The Cat, the Rat, and Lovell our Dog/Do rule all England, under the Hog.'

**fond**  Foolish.

**foot-cloth**  Large ornamental cloth laid over the back of a horse and hanging down to the ground on each side.

**started** Some editions read 'startled'.

**shrift** Confession.

**grace** Notice the different senses of this word in these two lines. In the first line it means 'favour'.

**Who builds** i.e. the man who builds.

**in air of your good looks** On the airy foundation of men's favour.

**bootless** Useless.

## Act III Scene 5

Richard and Buckingham are at pains to produce an atmosphere of crisis and are enjoying the task. They justify the execution of Hastings to the Lord Mayor and pretend that the haste with which it was carried out was contrary to their wishes. The Mayor departs to inform the citizens of their 'just proceedings' in this matter, and Richard sends Buckingham after him to proclaim to them the illegitimacy of Edward IV's children, his cruelty and his sensuality, and even to hint that Edward himself was illegitimate. Richard makes plans to imprison the children of Clarence.

### Commentary

The references to acting (with their apparent hints of the *over-*acting of some Elizabethan tragedians) are highly appropriate, not only to this scene of superb play-acting, but to the play as a whole, stage-managed, as it were, by a character who declares at the outset, 'Plots have I laid, inductions dangerous'. The short closing soliloquy (looking forward to IV,2, 8 ff) shows us that Buckingham is not yet privy to Richard's next plot.

**rotten** Rusted.

***ill-favoured*** Ugly. Richard and Buckingham are pretending that they are in danger of sudden attack from conspirators.

**counterfeit** Imitate.

**deep tragedian** Experienced tragic actor.

**intending** Pretending.

**offices** Functions.

**o'erlook** Inspect.

**plainest harmless** Most clearly innocent.

**book** Note-book.

**daub'd** Covered with a pleasing exterior, lit. plastered.

**omitted** Excepted.

**conversation** Sexual intimacy.

**from . . . suspects** Free from all taint of suspicion. The whole of this hypocritical speech is, of course, for the benefit of the Lord Mayor.

**covert'st shelter'd**  Most secretly camouflaged. As in 'plainest harmless' above, the superlative has almost the function of an adverb.

**almost**  Even.

**rashly**  Hastily (with none of the modern sense of recklessness).

**had we not determin'd . . . until**  It was not our intention that he should die before.

**have prevented**  Has anticipated, forestalled.

**Misconstrue us in him**  Misinterpret our actions towards him. Some editions read 'misconster' (an alternative spelling).

**As well as**  As well as if.

**of our intent**  For our plans.

**witness . . . intend**  Tell others what our plans were.

**your meet'st advantage of the time.**  The most advantageous moment you can find.

**Infer**  Allege. The Duchess of York, who objected to Edward's match with Lady Elizabeth Grey, tried to persuade Lady Elizabeth Lucy to say that she had been privately married to the king. But when this lady was put on oath she confessed that no such marriage had taken place. Buckingham, however, chose to ignore this and in his speech to the citizens declared that 'the children of King Edward the fourth were never lawfully begotten, for so much as the king (leaving his very wife Dame Elizabeth Lucy) was never lawfully married unto the queen their mother'.

**put to death a citizen**  The chroniclers tell how a merchant named Burdet, who lived 'at the sign of the Crown' in Cheapside, told his son that he would make him inheritor of 'the Crown', meaning his own house, 'but these words King Edward made to be misconstrued and interpreted that Burdet meant the crown of the realm'. The custom of giving houses and shops descriptive signs and not numbers continued in London until the middle of the eighteenth century.

**luxury**  Lasciviousness.

**change**  Fickleness. Edward IV was notorious for his pursuit of women.

**for a need**  If necessary, at a pinch.

**the golden fee**  i.e. the crown

**Baynard's Castle**  This had been the London house of Richard's father. It had been built by a Norman nobleman, Baynard, who came over with William the Conqueror. It was situated on the north bank of the Thames, near to the present Blackfriars Bridge, and was destroyed in the Great Fire of 1666.

**Doctor Shaa . . . Friar Penker**  Most editions read 'Shaw' for 'Shaa'. Holinshed describes how Richard and Buckingham tried to win the citizens to their side. 'Of spiritual men they took such as had wit, and were in authority among the people for opinion of their learning, and had no scrupulous conscience. Among these had they John Shaw, clerk, brother to the Mayor, and Friar Penker, provincial of the Augustine Friars, both Doctors of Divinity, both great preachers, both

of more learning than virtue, of more fame than learning.' These are
the two 'bishops' who appear in III,7.
**take some privy order**  Make some secret plans.

## Act III Scene 6

In a soliloquy the Scrivener who wrote the proclamation of
Hastings's death comments on the wickedness of the proceedings but realizes that no one is bold enough to protest against it.

### *Commentary*

The scene allows time for Buckingham to make his speech to the
citizens before reporting to Richard. Like II,3, it also indicates
that the people are far from being enthusiastic supporters of
Richard but are powerless to do anything but acquiesce. In this
way it provides a close link with the scene which follows.

*Scrivener*  A professional scribe who drew up legal documents.
**set hand**  The style of handwriting used for legal documents.
**fairly**  In its final form (cf. 'fair copy').
**engross'd**  Written in the large formal script appropriate to documents;
  hence, put into legal form.
**the sequel**  What follows.
**precedent**  The original draft, as distinct from the fair copy.
**untainted**  Not accused. The scrivener had been asked to prepare the
  document long before Hastings had been arrested.
**gross**  Stupid.
**Who is . . . palpable device**  In his *History,* More says that one citizen,
  realizing that a document issued two hours after Hastings's death must
  have taken a much longer time to prepare, observed 'that it was
  written by prophecy'.
**bold**  Some editions read 'blind'.
**naught**  Most editions read 'nought'. For the distinction see note on
  'naught', p.25.
**in thought**  Silently, without sign or protest.

## Act III Scene 7

Buckingham reports to Richard at Baynard's Castle that he has
not been able to rouse the citizens into accepting Richard as
king, and the two dukes plan how they will play their parts
before the Mayor. When the Mayor and citizens arrive Richard
sends a message that he is occupied in religious meditation, but
later he appears between two bishops to listen to Buckingham's

plea that he should take the throne. Urging his own unworthiness and saying that Edward V will in time prove a good king, Richard plays out the comedy as long as he can and finally says he must willingly accept the burden they lay upon him.

## Commentary

The scene is a further example of Shakespeare's consummate stagecraft. Richard and Buckingham enjoy their play-acting with great relish and Buckingham delights in carrying his rhetoric and inflated platitudes almost to the point of farce.

**Lady Lucy** See note on 'infer', p.49.

**contract . . . France** Warwick was sent to the court of Louis XI of France to arrange a marriage between Edward and Bona of Savoy, the sister-in-law of Louis. But when Warwick returned Edward had already become betrothed to Lady Elizabeth Grey.

**enforcement** Violation.

**tyranny for trifles** See note on 'put to death a citizen', p.49.

**infer** See note p.49.

**lineaments** Features.

**right idea** True image.

**victories** In 1482 Richard commanded an army that invaded Scotland and captured Berwick, which had previously been part of Scotland and has ever since remained English.

**discipline** Training, experience.

**statues** Most editions retain the original Elizabethan form of this word, 'statuas', pronounced with three syllables.

**breathing stones** Exactly like stones except that they breathed.

**Recorder** An official with legal knowledge appointed by the mayor and aldermen to 'record' or keep in mind the proceedings of their courts and the customs of the city.

**in warrant from himself** On his own responsibility.

**vantage** Advantage.

**Argues** Proves.

**intend** See note on 'intending', p.48.

**but by mighty suit** Except by earnest entreaty.

**And stand . . . churchmen** Buckingham seems to have forgotten that the idea originally came from Richard! See III,5.

**ground** Theme. The metaphor is from music, lit. plain-song or bass, on which a series of variations (descant) is sung or played.

**maid's part** Cf. the old proverb, 'Maids say nay and take it.'

**them** i.e. requests.

**leads** Flat roof covered with lead. In the Elizabethan theatre the actor playing Richard would mount to the balcony. See p.11.

**dance attendance** Wait obsequiously.

**withal** See note p.25.

**Divinely** Devoutly.

**exercise** See note p.45.

**deep divines** Experienced clergymen.

**watchful** Wakeful, unsleeping.

**beads** Prayers. This is the original meaning of the word. It was then applied to the parts of the rosary, by which prayers were counted, and finally to the components of a necklace.

**'tis much** It is a serious matter.

**fall of vanity** i.e. the downfall that awaits vanity.

**disgracious** Displeasing.

**state . . . birth** The position to which fortune has called you and to which your birth entitles you.

**lineal** Possessed by right of descent.

**doth want . . . limbs** Is lacking a suitable or necessary component part (or member).

**graft** The correct past participle, since the verb was originally 'to graff'. In his sermon to the citizens Dr Shaw took as his text, 'Bastard slips shall never take deep root.'

**shoulder'd in** Pushed into.

**recure** Remedy.

**factor** Agent.

**successively** By right of succession.

**from blood to blood** Handed on from one relation to another.

**empery** Dominion, empire.

**consorted with** In association with.

**yielded** Assented.

**fondly** See note on 'fond', p.47.

**season'd** Rendered agreeable.

**check'd** Should rebuke.

**Definitively** Decidedly.

**even** Smooth.

**ripe revenue** Possession due to me and ready to be enjoyed.

**bark . . . sea** A vessel unfit for the mighty ocean.

**Than . . . hid** Than wish to be rid of the responsibility of high position once I have assumed it.

**much I need** I much lack the ability.

**defend** Forbid.

**respects thereof** Considerations on which your attitude is based.

**nice** Over-subtle.

**contract** Betrothed. See note on 'infer', p.49. 'Contract' is a past participle, with the stress on the second syllable.

**substitute** Proxy. See note on 'contract . . . France', p.51.

**sister** i.e. sister-in-law.

**petitioner** Edward first met Lady Elizabeth Grey when she came to him to sue for her husband's lands.

**a many** Cf. the modern usage in 'a few', 'a good many'.

**prize and purchase** Capture.

**Seduc'd . . . bigamy** Tempted him to do that which was unworthy of his high position by marrying one who was far below him in rank and who had been married before. 'Pitch', a term from falconry, means the highest point in a bird's flight. According to the law of the church bigamy included marriage with a widow.

**whom our manners call** Whom we call by courtesy.

**some alive** i.e. the Duchess of York.

**I give . . . tongue** In order to spare their feelings I say nothing.

**benefit of dignity** Bestowal of the right of sovereignty.

**draw forth** Rescue.

**From . . . abusing times** From the admixture of base blood which has in recent times brought dishonour upon your true ancestry.

**Unto . . . course** To the proper line of descent.

**effeminate remorse** Tender pity.

**equally** Most editions retain the original spelling, 'egally'.

**estates** Ranks.

**Come, citizens** In some editions this line reads, 'Come, citizens: we will entreat no more.'

**'zounds** This oath is a corruption of 'God's wounds' – the kind of blasphemous oath that was fairly common in the Middle Ages. The form ' 'zounds' dates from 1600 and it was contracted to keep within the law that forbade the use of the name of God on the stage.

**imposition** The burden you lay upon me.

**Your mere enforcement** The mere fact that you have forced me.

**acquittance** Acquit.


## Revision questions on Act III

**1** From Scene 1 collect as many examples as you can of remarks which are full of irony.

**2** Suggest reasons why *Richard III* should contain as many as four children.

**3** How many remarks in Scene 2 have a double meaning for the reader or the audience?

**4** What aspects of Hastings's character are revealed in Act III?

**5** What do you learn from Act III of the attitude of the citizens of London to Richard's activities?

**6** Discuss the character of Buckingham as it is revealed in Act III.

**7** Discuss the skill with which Richard and Buckingham act their parts before the Mayor and citizens in Scenes 5 and 7.


## Act IV Scene 1

Queen Elizabeth, the Duchess of York, Anne and other members of the house of York wish to visit the young Princes but are refused admission to the Tower. Lord Stanley brings them news that Richard has seized the throne and that he sends for Anne to prepare for the coronation. Recalling her meeting with Richard at the funeral of Henry VI (I,2), Anne describes the misery she has endured as Richard's wife. Dorset prepares to join Richmond in France, with Stanley's blessing, and before going to sanctuary Queen Elizabeth prays that the Tower will treat her babies kindly.

## Commentary

After the success of Richard's cruelty and cunning, Shakespeare turns to the victims of that success and shows us their sufferings.

**niece** Granddaughter. This meaning was quite common until about 1600.

**aunt of Gloucester** Richard married Anne in 1472.

**for my life** Upon my life!

**gratulate** Greet.

**in law** By marriage.

**take thy office from thee** i.e. take on your office.

**two fair queens** Elizabeth and Anne, her two daughters-in-law.

**cross** Most editions omit the comma before this word and take it as an adverb meaning 'across'.

**Richmond** After the Battle of Tewkesbury, Richmond had taken refuge in Brittany.

**thrall** Slave.

**counted** Accounted, acknowledged.

**son** i.e. stepson. See note on 'Countess Richmond', p.31.

**ill-dispersing** Spreading evil.

**bed of death** The birthplace of death (i.e. of Richard, the cause of so many deaths).

**cockatrice** See note on 'basilisks', p.29

**unavoided** i.e. if not avoided.

**inclusive verge** Encircling rim, i.e. the crown that she will wear at her coronation.

**round** Surround. Steevens, an eighteenth-century editor of Shakespeare, sees Anne's words as an allusion to 'the ancient mode of punishing a regicide or any other egregious criminal, viz. by placing a crown of iron, heated red-hot, upon his head'.

**anointed** After referring to the crown she alludes to the holy oil with which she will be consecrated at her coronation.

**to feed my humour** To please me in my unhappy mood.

**so old a widow** As she was young (fifteen) at the time of Prince Edward's death she had many years of widowhood before her.

**Grossly** See note on 'gross', p.50.

**complaining eighty-odd years** See note 'complaints', p39. The Duchess
 was actually sixty-eight at this time. Shakespeare exaggerates her age to
 deepen the pathos of her position.
**teen** Grief.
**envy** See note on 'envious', p.35.
**ragged** Rugged, rough.
**use my babies well** In the very next scene Richard orders their deaths.


## Act IV Scene 2

Richard, now King but fearing his glory may not last, plans to kill
the Princes. Because Buckingham hesitates to support his
master's plan, Richard decides to cast him off and arranges with
Tyrrel the murder of the Princes. Stanley announces Dorset's
flight to Richmond, and Richard elaborates further plans – he will
arrange a mean marriage for Clarence's daughter; he plans to
bring about Anne's death and then marry Edward's daughter.
When Buckingham returns to claim the earldom of Hereford,
Richard at first ignores him and then makes it clear that he has no
further use for him. Buckingham decides to flee to Wales.


### *Commentary*

This scene marks the climax of Richard's fortunes and at the same
time foreshadows his downfall. Richmond's party is gaining
strength, while Richard is impelled by feelings of insecurity,
suspicion and even superstition to commit further crimes. He is
conscious that his kingdom 'stands on brittle glass' and that he has
proceeded 'so far in blood that sin will pluck on sin'.

*sennet* See note on p.44.
*in pomp* Dressed in splendour, or perhaps with a ceremonial
 procession.
**play the touch** Act like a touchstone. This was a hard stone used for
 testing the amount of gold or silver in alloys by the colour of the streak
 produced when they were rubbed on it. The metaphor is continued in
 'current', meaning 'genuine'.
**consequence** Sequel. Richard bitterly interprets the three words which
 Buckingham has just spoken as a continuation of his own previous
 remark, i.e. 'but Edward lives, (a) true (and) noble prince'. Most editors
 have found some difficulty in punctuating the next line so as to bring out
 Richard's meaning, that Edward still lived as the legitimate heir. The best
 method is that of the Quartos and Folio, which have no punctuation at all!
 – 'That Edward still should live true noble prince.' Richard similarly
 mocks Stanley by deliberately misinterpreting his words in IV,4, 476.

**suddenly** See note on 'sudden', p.34.

**resolve** Answer, inform.

**iron-witted** Stupid, or perhaps unfeeling, hard-hearted (not like Buckingham, who is beginning to have scruples).

**unrespective** Thoughtless, unreflecting. The opposite of 'deep-revolving', a few lines later.

**considerate** Calculating.

**High-reaching** Ambitious.

**close exploit** Secret deed.

**haughty** Aspiring.

**deep-revolving** Deeply reflective.

**witty** Cunning, clever.

**held out** Kept up. The metaphor of these two lines is from hunting.

**take order . . . close** Make arrangements to have her strictly confined.

**foolish** i.e. an idiot.

**it stands . . . upon** It is of great importance to me.

**daughter** Edward IV's daughter, Elizabeth. Dover Wilson comments on the whole speech: 'These rapidly conceived and various projects, drawn from widely separated passages in Holinshed, create an effect at once of intellectual brilliance and of over-excitement.'

**pluck on** Draw after it.

**deal upon** Deal with.

**no more but so** No more than that (i.e. what Richard has just whispered to Tyrrel).

**prefer** Advance, raise in rank or fortune.

**pawn'd** Pledged.

**peevish** See note p.33.

**How chance** How does it happen that.

**him** i.e. the prophet (Henry VI).

**Rougemont** This castle in Exeter was built by the order of William the Conqueror. The names 'Rougemont' and 'Richmond' may have had a similar pronunciation in Shakespeare's day.

**jack** The mechanical figure which struck the bell for the hours in old clocks. There is probably also a suggestion of the other meaning of this word. See note p.31.

**keep'st the stroke** Keep on striking (i.e. you are interrupting my thoughts with your continual demands).

**Brecknock** Buckingham had a manor at Brecknock (i.e. Brecon), in Wales.

**fearful** Literally full of fear.


## Act IV Scene 3

Tyrrel describes the murder of the Princes. Richard congratulates himself on the success of his schemes and on the death of Anne, and prepares to woo his brother's daughter Elizabeth. Catesby brings news that the Bishop of Ely has fled to

Richmond and that Buckingham has raised an army. Richard prepares to fight.

## Commentary

The unexpected poetry of Tyrrel's description increases our pity at the children's fate, while at the same time 'distancing' us from the physical act. The remorse of the murderers is an invented touch on Shakespeare's part.

**bloody act** Notice how the rather rhetorical pathos of Tyrrel's speech, and the remorse of Dighton and Forrest, intensify the audience's pity for the Princes and horror at Richard's evil. Whether Richard was in actual fact responsible for the murder of the Princes in the Tower is a question that will probably never be answered with certainty. The only definite facts are that the Duke of York joined the young King Edward V in the Tower on 16 June 1483, and that neither of them was ever seen again outside the Tower. How and why they died is certainly not known. Many writers have argued that Richard had nothing to gain and much to lose by murdering them, and some have laid the responsibility for their deaths on Henry VII, who had a great deal to gain thereby. Studies of the problem make fascinating reading; but Shakespeare's Richard is the Richard of the Tudor chroniclers. See p.17.

**arch** Pre-eminent.

**piece** Perhaps here in the sense of 'masterpiece' – a meaning which is found elsewhere in the 16th century. Some editors follow the First Quarto, which has 'this ruthless piece of butchery'. The Sixth Quarto has 'this ruthful piece of butchery' and the Folio reads 'this piece of ruthful butchery'.

**flesh'd** Inured to bloodshed, hardened. A metaphor from hunting. To 'flesh' a hound or falcon was to reward it with a piece of the flesh of the first game it killed.

**in their death's sad story** In telling how they died.

**alabaster** i.e. like marble. The association is with a carved figure on a tomb.

**replenished** Complete, perfect.

**prime** First.

**gone** Some editions read 'Thus both are gone', perhaps in the sense of 'overwhelmed, overcome' (rather than of 'gone away').

**soon at after-supper** Towards 'late supper' – the light meal that commonly followed supper.

**process** Story.

**inheritor** Possessor.

**pent up** Confined.

**Abraham's bosom** The abode of departed spirits. See Luke, 16, 22.

**bid the world good night** Anne died on 16 March 1485.

**Breton** Richmond was in exile (not born) in Brittany.

**aims** Richmond had sworn that if he gained the throne he would marry Elizabeth.

**looks proudly on** Looks with a haughty eye towards. Some editions read 'looks proudly o'er', i.e. as if he already regarded it as his own.

**Morton** i.e. the Bishop of Ely, who had been put into Buckingham's custody at Brecknock.

**is in the field** Has begun military operations.

**power** Army.

**fearful . . . delay** Timorous discussion leads only to delay.

**leads . . . beggary** Leads to helpless and sluggish ruin.

**fiery . . . wing** Speedy action must carry me through.

**Mercury** See note p.38.

**my counsel is my shield** The only friend I shall confide in is my shield, or the only help I require is that of my shield.

**We must . . . field** i.e. there is no time for talking when traitors defy us by fighting.

## Act IV Scene 4

Queen Margaret, lurking to watch the gradual destruction of all the enemies of the house of Lancaster, is joined by Queen Elizabeth and the Duchess of York. The three vie with one another in lamentation and join in heaping curses on Richard. When Richard enters he drowns their accusations with the noise of trumpets and drums. Before she departs his mother pronounces a solemn curse upon him. In a long scene of artificial and antithetical verse Richard endeavours to win over Queen Elizabeth to woo her daughter for him. Ratcliffe brings news of the appearance of Richmond's fleet off the coast; for a moment Richard seems confused and his orders are far from clear. When Stanley brings further news of Richmond, Richard suspects Stanley's loyalty and commands him to leave his son as a hostage before mustering an army. Messengers bring news of more risings, of the flight and capture of Buckingham after the dispersal of his army, and of the landing of Richmond's army in Wales.

## *Commentary*

The scene with Queen Elizabeth poses an important question. Does she really consent to the marriage of her daughter with the man who has murdered two of her sons? In the next scene (IV,5) we learn from Stanley that she has agreed to her daughter's betrothal with Richmond, and one school of thought holds that Elizabeth deliberately deceived Richard. In Cibber's version (see p.21), after the words

I go. Write to me very shortly,
And you shall understand from me her mind.

she is given an 'aside' which indicates that she merely pretends to yield in order to gain time for Richmond's advance. Some critics argue that this scene almost exactly balances the wooing of Lady Anne (I,2), and that there Shakespeare shows Richard's success against almost impossible odds, whereas in this scene Richard, now approaching his end, is seen to be outwitted by a woman. On the other hand, we may explain the apparent discrepancy between IV,4 and 5 by accepting that this 'shallow, changing woman' first gave way to Richard and afterwards changed her mind and consented to the marriage of her daughter with Richmond. This interpretation would tally with the chroniclers, who comment on Elizabeth's inconstancy (although in the chronicles the sequence of events is reversed: having promised the princess to Richmond, she was afterwards persuaded by Richard to give her to him). Shakespeare may have intended to show us that Richard, having passed the height of his power, was hoodwinked by a woman's deceit in a situation in which he had previously triumphed; but the text certainly does not make his intention clear.

**Enter old Queen Margaret**  Notice the effectiveness of Margaret's first speech following immediately on the end of the previous scene. There would be no break between the scenes as presented in the Elizabethan theatre (see p.10).

**So, now . . . death.**  The image is of prosperity falling like a fruit through over-ripeness, while a skeleton is lying at the foot of the tree, waiting to devour the fruit.

**induction**  Preparation, lit. prologue to a play.

**consequence**  See note p.55.

**unblow'd**  Most editions read 'unblown', i.e. never grown to maturity, lit. (of flowers) still in the bud.

**new-appearing**  Only lately become visible, i.e. not very old. The adjective, together with 'sweets' (scented flowers), carries on the metaphor.

**doom**  Death, destruction.

**right for right**  Dr Johnson paraphrases this as 'justice answering to the claim for justice'. Given a wider application than in Margaret's sentence, the phrase might well be regarded as the theme of the play.

**infant morn**  i.e. the bright young lives of your infants.

**aged night**  The darkness that death brings, which is associated with old age, not infancy.

**craz'd** Cracked, broken.

**quit** Requite, repay.

**dying debt** A debt that could be paid only by death.

**Dead life, blind sight** Examples of oxymoron (see note on 'Literary terms', p.15), frequently used in Shakespeare's early plays to convey intense emotion. The Duchess applies these phrases to herself and goes on to describe herself as one who should be dead but is still alive, as the stage where woes are acted out, as one of whom the world is ashamed (because she gave birth to Richard), who should be in her grave but who is still in possession of life, and who sums up the experience of many weary years of life.

**thou** i.e. the earth.

**benefit of seigniory** Priority. 'Seigniory' (probably from 'seigneur') is lordship, sovereignty – i.e. superior feudal rank.

**frown on the upper hand** Take pride of place over yours.

**Thou hadst an Edward . . . Richard** i.e. Edward V and the young Duke of York. She is addressing Queen Elizabeth.

**I had a Richard too** i.e. her husband, the Duke of York, who was killed with his son Rutland at the battle of Wakefield.

**help'st** Helped.

**teeth** See note on 'they say', p.41.

**excellent** Pre-eminent.

**galled** Sore with weeping.

**carnal** Carnivorous, murderous.

**pew-fellow** Companion, lit. one who shares the same pew.

**cloy me** Satisfy my appetite (for revenge).

**Thy Edward** i.e. Edward IV.

**Thy other Edward** i.e. Edward V.

**but boot** Only a makeweight, an additional item thrown in .

**adulterate** Adulterous – because of his association with Jane Shore.

**intelligencer** Secret agent.

**only reserv'd . . . thither** The only reason why he has not yet been sent to Hell is that he may act as the agent of the powers of evil in buying human souls and sending them to Hell.

**bond of life** A legal metaphor. Cf. 'lease of life'.

**bottled . . . bunch-back'd** See notes p.33.

**vain flourish** See note p.33.

**presentation** Representation, show.

**index** Prologue.

**pageant** Scene or show on a stage. The modern sense of a brilliant or stately spectacle is not found before the nineteenth century. 'Shadow', 'painted', 'presentation', 'index' and 'pageant' are all theatrical metaphors.

**a-high** On high.

**only mock'd with** As though fortune gave her two children only to mock her by taking them away again. One of the earlier senses of 'to mock' was 'to tantalize'.

**sign** i.e. merely a symbol and nothing more.

**garish flag**  It has been suggested that the image is that of a standard-bearer with a showy flag which attracts the enemy's fire ('shot' = marksman). Perhaps a reference to Elizabeth's beauty being subject to the 'dangerous shots' of envy. The position of this line differs in some editions.

**to fill the scene**  To fill out the action (another theatrical metaphor).

**Decline**  Go through from beginning to end (as we decline nouns in learning Latin).

**caitiff**  Miserable wretch.

**scorn'd of**  Scorned by.

**fear'd of**  Feared by.

**one**  i.e. Richard.

**whirl'd about**  Come round in a circle.

**no more but thought**  Only the recollection.

**Bettering**  Exaggerating.

**Windy**  Full of talk (cf. 'long-winded'). This, with the adjective 'airy', implies that words, as distinct from actions, are mere breath, without substance.

**attorneys**  Advocates, pleaders. Originally the word 'attorney' meant 'one who acts on another's behalf'. Elizabeth means that words 'represent' woes, as a lawyer represents his client.

**succeeders . . . joys**  Another legal metaphor. 'Intestate' means 'without having made a will' (or 'testament'). The joys have died without having made a will because they have nothing to bequeath, so that words, the heirs, come into an empty inheritance.

**exclaims**  See note p.28.

**expedition**  March.

**ow'd**  Owned (as often in Shakespeare).

**Ned Plantagenet**  Cf. IV,3, 36.

**the Lord's anointed**  i.e. a king by divine right.

**entreat me fair**  Treat me well.

**clamorous report**  Noisy sounds.

**condition**  Disposition.

**Tetchy**  Fretful, peevish.

**age confirm'd**  i.e. maturity, when early traits become firmly established.

**kind in hatred**  i.e. Richard, hypocritically, could make his hatred appear to be kindness. No doubt there is a play on the other sense of 'kind' (natural) - i.e. Richard is cruel *by nature*.

**comfortable**  Comforting, cheering.

**Humphrey Hower**  No one has ever been able to explain this phrase satisfactorily. The Elizabethans used the phrase 'dining with Duke Humphrey' to mean 'going without a meal', since, while others dined, beggars loitered away the dinner-time in 'Duke Humphrey's Walk' (one of the aisles in old St Paul's Cathedral). The lines here may possibly mean that the only pleasure the Duchess gained in Richard's company was when she was leaving him to go to a meal.

**forth of**  Out of.

**disgracious** Ungracious.

**turn** Return.

**tire** i.e. may it tire. 'Fight', 'whisper' and 'promise' similarly express a wish – a wish that is fulfilled when Richard is visited by the ghosts of his victims before the Battle of Bosworth (V,3).

**adverse party** Opposing side.

**Whisper** i.e. may they whisper *to*.

**serves** Follows.

**doth attend** With the double meaning of 'waits *upon*' (i.e. serves) and 'waits *for*'.

**more** Some editions, following the Quartos, read 'moe'. 'Moe' was often used as the comparative of 'many', with 'more' as the comparative of 'much'.

**level** Aim.

**Wrong not her birth.** The dialogue that follows is another example of *sticomythia*. See note on 'Lady . . . Villain', p.28.

**opposite** See note p.39.

**unavoided** Unavoidable.

**avoided grace** Deliberate rejection of the grace of God i.e. Richard's wickedness.

**cozen'd** Cheated. Note the pun. 'Cozen' may just possibly be connected with 'cousin' by derivation, perhaps through a phrase like 'to call cousins', to pretend to be related to, hence to deceive. Cf. the French verb *cousiner*, one of the meanings of which is 'to sponge'.

**direction** Order, command.

**use of** Indulgence in.

**reft** Bereft.

**dangerous success** Hazardous issue. 'Success' originally meant result, good *or* bad.

**discover'd** *Un*covered, revealed.

**type** Sign, symbol, lit. distinguishing mark or badge. The whole phrase means 'the crown'.

**demise** Assign.

**Lethe** In classical mythology Lethe is one of the rivers of the underworld, the river of forgetfulness.

**process** See note on p.57.

**telling** i.e. in telling.

**date** Duration.

**from my soul** Richard uses the phrase in its normal sense, but the Queen changes its meaning by quibbling on another sense of 'from' – away from. She believes with all her heart that Richard's love for her daughter does not come from his heart.

**haply** Perhaps.

**handkerchief** See note on 'my father's death', p.29.

**sap** Blood.

**withal** See note p.25.

**Mad'st quick conveyance** Quickly got rid of in an underhand way.

**spoil** Havoc, destruction.

**shall deal unadvisedly**  Cannot help acting thoughtlessly.

**quicken your increase**  Give life to your progeny.

**doting**  Tender, fond.

**metal**  Substance.

**bid**  Endured, suffered (past tense of 'bide').

**but a son being king**  Only in respect of your son being king.

**orient**  Bright, lustrous, lit. coming from the east. Originally applied to Indian pearls, and then to any very lustrous pearls.

**Advantaging**  Adding to the value of.

**retail**  See note p.43.

**What were I best**  What would be best for me.

**That God . . . pleasing**  That would not seem impious, illegal, dishonourable to me and hateful to my daughter.

**vail**  Lower, i.e. yield.

**subject low**  Some editors, following the Quartos, read 'subject love', thus making an antithesis with 'loathes' in the next line. The twenty-eight lines of this exchange between Richard and Elizabeth provide another example of *sticomythia* (see note, p.15).

**quick**  Richard means 'hasty', but the Queen takes it in the sense of 'living'.

**George**  Part of the insignia of the Order of the Garter was a jewel bearing the figure of St George.

**his**  Its (in all three lines). Our usual form of the neuter possessive became common only after 1600. There is no reference here to Clarence.

**pawn'd . . . virtue**  Forfeited its power as a symbol of knighthood.

**That . . . time o'erpast**  You have wronged the future by filling it with the sorrow of those who have suffered from your wrongs in the past.

**Hereafter time**  The time to come.

**children**  She may be referring to Clarence's children.

**Ungovern'd youth**  Children with no one to guide them.

**in their age**  When they are old.

**with their age**  Together with their old age.

**by times ill-us'd o'erpast**  By making bad use of past time. Some editions read 'by time misus'd o'erpast', which has the same meaning.

**Myself myself confound!**  May I bring about my own destruction! The student will understand the meaning of these lines more clearly if he imagines that these words begin a new sentence, with a new construction which is linked to 'if', four lines later.

**tender**  See note on 'tend'ring', p.24.

**attorney**  See note p.61.

**peevish found**  Some editions read 'peevish-fond' (i.e. foolishly perverse), a conjecture by the 18th-century editor Malone.

**forget myself to be myself**  Forget that I am what I am, a mother whose children you have murdered.

**if your self's . . . yourself**  If, in playing the wronged mother, you neglect your duty as the mother of Elizabeth.

**nest of spicery**  A reference to the phoenix, a mythical bird which, after it had lived for five hundred years, died on a pyre of spices, from the ashes of which rose a new phoenix.

**recomforture** Renewed consolation.

**puissant** Powerful. The remainder of this scene is described by Dover Wilson as 'telescoped and kaleidoscoped history', for in it Shakespeare compresses a series of events which actually spread over two years (October 1483–August 1485).

**hull** Drift with furled sails.

**expecting but** Only waiting for.

**Dull, unmindful villain!** Richard's irritability and forgetfulness seem to show that he is losing his grip.

**power** See note p.58.

**suddenly** Quickly.

**Hoyday** An exclamation of surprise or impatience.

**White-liver'd runagate** Cowardly fugitive. The liver was supposed to be the seat of courage, and lack of blood would make it white. 'Runagate' is a corruption of 'renegade'.

**chair** i.e. the throne.

**is the sword unsway'd?** Is the sword of state, the symbol of royal power, not being wielded?

**What heir** i.e. what legitimate heir. Edward's daughter had been declared illegitimate, and the children of Clarence were debarred by the act of attainder against their father.

**Welshman** Richmond was the son of Edmund Tudor, the head of a great Welsh family. See note on 'Countess Richmond', p.31.

**in the north** Since the 14th century the Stanleys have been the chief family in Lancashire and Cheshire.

**I'll not trust thee** Richard was right in suspecting Stanley's loyalty. Although Stanley could not raise forces for his stepson, Richmond, his treachery at the Battle of Bosworth brought about Richard's downfall.

**assurance** Security.

**advertised** Informed. The word has four syllables here, with the stress on the second.

**The Guildfords** An important Kentish family.

**competitors** Partners, associates.

**owls** The cry of the owl was regarded as an omen of misfortune or death.

**fall of waters** Heavy rains.

**cry thee mercy** Beg your pardon.

**well-advised** Prudent.

**Sir Thomas Lovel** Not the Lord Lovell who appears briefly in III, 5.

**if . . . assistants** If they were going to support him.

**Hois'd** Hoisted.

**Bretagne** i.e. Brittany.

**Milford** Milford Haven, in Wales, where Richmond landed on 7 August 1485. His 'mighty power' consisted of only two thousand men!

**reason** Talk.

**royal battle** One which will decide who is to be king.

# Act IV Scene 5

Lord Stanley sends Richmond a message by a priest to say that he cannot help Richmond because Richard holds young Stanley as a hostage and that Queen Elizabeth has consented to her daughter's marriage with Richmond. Stanley learns the names of the important nobles who have joined Richmond's forces, which are now advancing towards London from Wales.

In some editions lines 6–8 of Stanley's first speech are, with slight variations, transferred to the beginning of his last speech.

## Commentary

The main purpose of this short scene is to transmit to the audience information which telescopes events of 1483 and 1485 and shows the increasing power of Richard's enemies. It also throws light on the character of Stanley, whom Holinshed described as 'a wilie fox'.

**Sir Christopher** See note on 'Sir John', p.45. Urswick was a priest, confessor to the Countess of Richmond, and used by her in communicating with her son when he was in exile. When Richmond became king, Urswick was appointed a chaplain and royal ambassador.

**frank'd up** See note p.34.

**name** Repute.

**Sir William Stanley** The brother of the Lord Stanley in the play.

**crew** Band (not used with the modern sense of disparagement). When Richmond left Wales he had an army of five thousand men. (See note on 'Milford', above.)

## Revision questions on Act IV

**1** Explain how Scene 1 brings together almost all those who suffer from Richard's cruel schemes.

**2** Show how Scene 2 is both the climax of Richard's success and the beginning of his end.

**3** Describe the part played by Lord Stanley in Act IV.

**4** What is the dramatic purpose of the scene in which Queen Margaret, Queen Elizabeth and the Duchess of York appear together?

**5** What is your interpretation of the scene in which Richard attempts to gain Elizabeth's consent to his marriage with her daughter? Does he really succeed, or does she deceive him?

**6** Describe Richard's situation and his state of mind at the end of Scene 4.

## Act V Scene 1

At Salisbury Buckingham recalls Queen Margaret's prophecy as he is led off to be executed.

**Holy King Henry**  See note on 'invocate', p.27.
**moody**  Angry.
**determin'd . . . wrongs**  The fixed time to which the punishment of my wrongs has been postponed.
**feigned prayer**  See II,1, 32–40.
**Wrong . . . blame**  i.e. the evil that I have done has brought upon me the unjust death I now suffer. Here is another line which, given a wider application, might be said to sum up the implications of the whole play. See note on 'right for right', p.59.

## Act V Scene 2

Richmond addresses his troops at Tamworth. This is Richmond's first appearance in the play: he comes in God's name, 'to reap the harvest of perpetual peace'.

### Commentary

Though some critics see Richmond as invested with all the glory of the house of Tudor (which, as Henry VII, he was to found), there is little evidence of it in this scene.

With Richmond's appearance the play has clearly reached its final phase. Dr Johnson suggested that Act V should really begin with this scene.

**bowels**  Interior, i.e. 'the heart of the country'.
**father**  Stepfather.
**Lines**  i.e. the letter referred to in IV,5.
**boar**  See reference to 'rooting', p.33.
**spoil'd**  Pillaged, plundered.
**Swills**  Greedily gulps down.
**wash**  Scraps given to pigs, from the washing of kitchen dishes.
**embowell'd**  We should now say *dis*embowelled.
**Tamworth**  The chroniclers record that while Richard and his army were moving towards Leicester, Richmond marched from Shrewsbury to Lichfield and then on to Tamworth, a town on the boundary of Staffordshire and Warwickshire. Bosworth, near which the battle was fought, is almost exactly halfway between Tamworth and Leicester.
**cheerly**  Cheerfully.

**a thousand men**  For 'men' some editions read 'swords'. It is
  interesting to note that Richard, waking from a troubled sleep after
  the visits of the ghosts, uses a similar image, 'My conscience hath a
  thousand several tongues.'

## Act V Scene 3

The tents of Richard and Richmond are pitched at Bosworth
Field and the two leaders make final preparations for the coming battle. Richmond sends a message to Lord Stanley, whose
forces lie somewhat apart from the two armies. Richard also
sends him a message, commanding that his forces join the King's
army by sunrise. Stanley visits Richmond in his tent, promising
that he will give him all the help he can by temporizing in the
battle. Richmond prays, asking for God's favour on his forces as
'ministers of chastisement'. While both leaders sleep they are
visited by the ghosts of Richard's victims – Prince Edward,
Henry VI, Clarence, Rivers, Grey and Vaughan, Hastings, the
two young Princes, Lady Anne and Buckingham – who bid
Richard despair and die, and Richmond live and flourish.
Richard wakes in confusion after his 'fearful dream'; Richmond
is cheerful after a sound sleep and makes an encouraging speech
to his soldiers. Richard comes from eavesdropping among his
soldiers' tents, draws up the plan of battle and speaks stirringly
to his army. He receives news that Stanley has refused to support him.

## Commentary

Notice how Shakespeare uses the simple stage arrangements of
his own time. The two leaders enter alternately on either side
and discuss their plans in almost exactly the same spot; their
tents are within a few feet of each other; and inside their tents
both Richard and Richmond are throughout in full view of the
audience. Yet this very simplicity has advantages – for example,
the alternate curses and blessings of the ghost are much more
effective if the two leaders are sleeping close together.

**ha!**  Eh?
**all's one for that**  Never mind that.
**battalia**  A large armed force in battle array. The word is a doublet of
  'battle', which was often used to mean 'army' (it occurs three times in this
  sense later in this same scene and elsewhere in the play); it is connected
  with the word 'battalion'. Some editions have 'battalion' here.

**account** Number.

**vantage** Condition favourable to success.

**direction** Ability in directing soldiers.

**discipline** See note p.51.

**token of a goodly day** For 'token' some editions read 'signal'. Contrast lines 283–8 of this scene. Though Shakespeare is apparently somewhat inconsistent, meteorologically speaking, he makes good dramatic use of the weather – the sky shines on Richmond and frowns on Richard.

**keeps** Remains with.

**form and model** Plan of military formation.

**Limit** Appoint, assign.

**part** Divide.

**beaver** Helmet. Strictly speaking, a beaver is the face-guard of a helmet.

**blind** Dark.

**watch** Either (a) a sentinel, or (b) a watch-light, a candle marked in sections by the burning of which one could count the hours.

**white Surrey** Shakespeare invents this name for the 'great white courser' on which, according to Holinshed, Richard had entered Leicester.

**staves** Shafts of lances. Knights carried two or three spare lances into battle.

**melancholy** Sullen. Richard suspected Northumberland's loyalty. In actual fact Northumberland held aloof 'with a great company and intermitted not'. After the battle he was rewarded by Richmond.

**cockshut time** Twilight. Either (a) the time when poultry are shut up, or (b) the time when woodcock 'shoot' through the glades of a wood and can be caught by nets stretched across the opening.

**father-in-law** Stepfather.

**flaky** Broken with streaks of light.

**Prepare thy battle** Draw up your army.

**mortal-staring** Glaring fatally.

**With best advantage** Making the best use of any favourable opportunity.

**deceive the time** Play for time.

**tender George** Shakespeare follows the chroniclers in making George Stanley a boy, although he was in fact a married man at the time of the Battle of Bosworth.

**leisure** Time at our disposal. The word has the same sense four lines later.

**troubled thoughts** The Quartos have 'troubled noise', and some editors prefer this, since Richmond is throughout unusually calm. (He is addressed by the ghost of Hastings as 'quiet, untroubled soul'.)

**peise** Weigh.

**bruising** Crushing (referring to the heavy iron maces used in battle).

**watchful** Wakeful, unsleeping.

**windows** i.e. eyelids.

*Ghost*  Shakespeare may have got the idea of introducing the ghosts
from Holinshed. The ghosts appear in the order in which they met
their deaths, thus providing a résumé of the whole story of Richard's
crimes. Some critics are unhappy about the style of the ghosts'
speeches, which they regard as ineffective, and believe that these may
have been added by another hand than Shakespeare's; or Shakespeare
may have deliberately written them in the rather flat style associated
with pageants. 'It gives the Ghosts the proper symbolic quality by
helping us to forget the sort of people they were when they were alive'
(M. M. Reese, *The Cease of Majesty*).

**punched**  Pierced.

**prophesied**  See IV,2, 99.

**wash'd . . . wine**  Drowned with an excess of wine.

**fall**  Let fall.

**edgeless**  i.e. which will, as a result, be able to do no injury.

**annoy**  Injury.

**for hope**  The precise meaning of this phrase has been disputed. It
could be (a) 'for want of hope' (i.e. from despair), or (b) 'hoping to give
you aid (but I died before I could do so).'

**fight**  i.e. are fighting (not 'may they fight').

**fall**  The Folio has 'fall' (i.e. let him fall); the Quartos have 'falls'. The
particular reading adopted will determine the interpretation of 'fight'
in the previous line.

**horse . . . wounds**  Buckingham's words (1. 172) are true: Richard
wakes from a dream of 'bloody deeds and death', in which he believes
that his horse has been killed under him – a good dramatic touch in
view of what happens later. One is also reminded that Clarence had a
'fearful dream' just before his death.

**lights burn blue**  This was believed to be the sign of the presence of a
ghost.

**I and I**  This is the reading adopted by the Arden editor, who follows
the first Quarto, with not very convincing reasoning. Every other
editor accepts the reading of the later Quartos and the First Folio, 'I
am I'. This is an echo of part of Richard's famous soliloquy in *Henry
VI, Part 3*, just after he has murdered Henry VI in the Tower: 'And
this word 'love', which greybeards call divine,/Be resident in men like
one another/And not in me: I am myself alone.'

**I am a villain**  Cf. Richard's opening soliloquy ('I am determined to
prove a villain').

**several**  See note p.45.

**Perjury**  i.e. on the part of the tongue of conscience.

**us'd**  Committed habitually.

**shadows**  Ratcliffe uses the word in the sense of 'illusions, things that
are not real', Richard with the additional sense of 'departed spirits'.
See note p.35.

**proof**  Armour, especially armour that has been proved and tested.

**come, go with me**  Notice how this device leaves room on the stage for
the entrance of Richmond's soldiers.

**fairest-boding** Prophesying pleasant things.

**cried on** Called out.

**soul** Some editions have the Folio reading, 'heart'.

***Richmond's oration*** The orations of both Richmond and Richard are based on Holinshed.

**enforcement** Constraint.

**made means** Contrived a way.

**stone . . . precious . . . foil . . . set** All four words develop the same image, with an additional quibble on 'set' (seated). A foil was a thin leaf of metal placed under a precious stone to increase its brilliance, or under some transparent substance to make it appear a precious stone.

**ward** Guard (the same word in another form).

**fat** Richness, abundance.

**age** i.e. old age.

**Advance** Raise.

**ransom** The penalty of failure.

**What said Northumberland** Richard and Ratcliffe are discussing what they have overheard during their eavesdropping. See line 222, and note on 'melancholy', p.68.

**Tell the clock** Count the strokes.

**by the book** According to the calendar

**brav'd** Made glorious.

**lour** Look angry.

**from** Away from.

**vaunts** Exults.

**Caparison** Cover with rich trappings.

**foreward** Vanguard.

**main battle** Principal division of the army.

**puissance** Force.

**Jockey** A familiar form of 'Jack' or 'John'.

**bought and sold** Betrayed for a bribe.

**babbling dreams** Richard has now recovered from the mood of lines 179–206. It was at this point that Cibber (see p.21) made him say, 'Richard's himself again'.

**pell-mell** Fighting hand to hand, at close quarters.

**inferr'd** Alleged.

**sort** Set, gang, chance collection.

**lackey** Hanging-on, as camp followers.

**o'er-cloyed** Over-filled, over-populated.

**restrain** Withhold. This is the reading of the Quartos and Folio, but some editors have suggested *distrain* (seize).

**distain** Stain (i.e. defile).

**Bretagne** i.e. Brittany. Some editions have 'Britaine'.

**brother's** This is the Arden editor's correction of 'mother's', found in the Quartos and the First Folio. During his exile Richmond was supported by Richard's *brother*-in-law, the Duke of Burgundy. The mistake is due to a printer's error in the second edition of Holinshed, which is the edition Shakespeare must have used.

**whip these stragglers**  A reference to the penalty imposed by law upon vagabonds in Shakespeare's time. They were to be soundly whipped by the beadle before being sent back to their home town.

**overweening**  Presumptuous.

**bobb'd**  Buffeted.

**in record**  Some editors, following the later Quartos, read 'on record'. Both phrases mean 'as is recorded'.

**Amaze . . . staves**  i.e. fight so fiercely that you frighten the sky with the splinters flying through the air from your broken lances. See note on 'staves', p.68.

**past the marsh**  Richmond no longer has his right flank covered by the marsh. Richard must engage with him immediately and has no time to deal with George Stanley.

**spleen**  The spleen was regarded as the seat of anger.

## Act V Scene 4

Richard performs wonders in battle and fights on courageously even when his horse is slain.

### *Commentary*

Stage-entry on horseback being impracticable, Shakespeare invented the idea that Richard's horse should have been slain under him.

**Daring an opposite**  If this means anything it could be interpreted as 'challenging an opponent'. Some editors adopt a suggestion of Tyrwhitt, an 18th-century editor, 'daring and opposite (i.e. boldly confronting), which is obviously better sense.

**A horse! . . . a horse!**  This famous line was much parodied by 17th-century dramatists.

**cast**  Throw of a dice i.e. this one battle. 'Die' in the following line is the singular of 'dice'. (Today we treat 'dice' as singular.)

## Act V Scene 5

The climax of the battle is reached when Richard and Richmond meet face to face and Richard is killed. Stanley, whose son is now safe, enters with the crown, which he places on Richmond's head, and Richmond announces that he will 'unite the white rose and the red' by marrying Elizabeth and will 'enrich the time to come with smooth-fac'd peace'.

## Commentary

The stage directions of the original editions are not as full as we could have wished. It is not even clear whether Shakespeare intended Richard's death to be enacted on stage, and some modern editions have the direction, 'Enter from opposite sides King Richard and Richmond, and exeunt fighting'. This would solve the problem of getting Richard's body off stage and fit in with Richmond's re-entry and Stanley's bearing the crown. The Arden editor discusses the matter at some length, and most modern productions bring out the full symbolic significance of the play's final encounter between good and evil by showing us Richard's death. An Elizabethan audience, however, may well have been more interested in the speeches of Richmond as the founder of the Tudor dynasty. Bernard Shaw called them 'pious twaddle' but Tillyard said of Richmond, 'He gets everything right and refers to all the things an Elizabethan audience cared about.'

**King Richard and Richmond** Holinshed tells how Richard eventually met his rival and had engaged him in personal conflict when Sir William Stanley (Lord Stanley's brother) suddenly attacked with 3,000 men. Richard was overwhelmed and 'manfully fighting in the middle of his enemies, was slain'. Some editions make the final section of the play into a separate scene; and in these V. 5 begins at this point. In the First Folio there are only two scenes in the Act, the second beginning as in our texts.

**the bloody dog is dead** Cf. IV, 4, 78. Shakespeare has already stretched historical probability by introducing Queen Margaret into his play at all (see note on 'banished', p.32). He could hardly make her 'live to say, The dog is dead!' but he makes effective use of this echo of her words.

**acquit thee** Acquitted thyself.

**royalty** Emblem of royalty i.e. the crown.

**ta'en the sacrament** i.e. previously sworn. See note on 'aims', p.58.

**the white rose and the red** The emblems of the houses of York and Lancaster.

**that long have frown'd** Some editions read 'hath'. 'That' refers to 'heaven', which was often treated as a plural. Cf. I.3.219.

**All this** This is the reading of the Quartos and Folio, but Dr Johnson suggested changing 'this' to 'that', so that the sentence meant, 'Let them unite all that York and Lancaster divided'.

**smooth-fac'd** i.e. free from care and anxiety.

**Abate the edge** Lessen the power to wound, lit. blunt the sword.

**reduce** Bring back.

**civil wounds** i.e. the devastation caused by civil war.

**Revision questions on Act V**

1 Discuss Shakespeare's presentation of Richmond. Do you think he is a sufficiently 'mighty opposite' to Richard? Does Shakespeare invest him with any more than human power?

2 Compare and contrast the orations which the two leaders make to their respective armies.

3 Why does Shakespeare introduce the ghosts of Richard's victims?

4 Summarize Richard's train of thought in his speech immediately after he awakens from his 'fearful dream'.

# Shakespeare's art in *Richard III*

## Setting

*Richard III* takes place historically in the late fifteenth century, but we are never very far from the London Shakespeare knew while he was writing the play in the reign of the Earl of Richmond's granddaughter, and his audience would be familiar with the very buildings which provided the setting for many of his scenes and references – Crosby Place, Baynard's Castle, the Guildhall, the Carmelite priory of White-Friars, Westminster Abbey with its sanctuary, the Bishop of Ely's house in Holborn, the Tower, popularly held to have been built by Julius Caesar, and Tower Bridge, where traitors' heads were placed on public view. The play also contains references to morality plays ('the formal Vice, Iniquity', III,1), to the popular sport of falconry, to the strolling clown with the monkey on his shoulder (III,1), and to the penalty imposed by Elizabethan law on vagabonds ('whip these stragglers', V,3).

## Theme and structure

The story of the play is the rise and fall of a tyrant ('One raised in blood, and one in blood established'), but woven into this story is a pattern of events that may be viewed from many angles. At its simplest it is a story of crime and punishment. On another level the pattern may be seen as part of the whole historical cycle which began in *Henry VI, Part I* – the culmination of the thirty years of civil war which we call the Wars of the Roses, and the expiation of a whole sequence of evil, inherited from the past and involving by turns the houses of Lancaster and York. This is the pattern which pleased the Tudor historians who provided Shakespeare with his material (see 'Sources', p.17), and this is in the Duchess of York's mind when she says:

Accursed and unquiet wrangling days,
How many of you have mine eyes beheld!
My husband lost his life to get the crown;
And often up and down my sons were toss'd,
For me to joy and weep their gain and loss:

And being seated, and domestic broils
Clean over-blown, themselves, the conquerors,
Make war upon themselves; brother to brother,
Blood to blood, self against self: O! preposterous
And frantic outrage, end thy damned spleen. (II.4)

Disorder breeds disorder, injustice leads to further injustice; each crime calls for vengeance and leads to further crime until it seems that the sequence will never end. The house of York has all but destroyed the house of Lancaster and it seems that order will be re-established only by the complete destruction of the house of York itself. This is what Queen Elizabeth foresees in II,4:

Ay me! I see the ruin of my House! . . .
Insulting tyranny begins to jut
Upon the innocent and aweless throne:
Welcome, destruction, blood, and massacre!
I see, as in a map, the end of all.

But the pattern of the play is more than a political one. At a deeper level the world of history is 'transformed into an intricate design of which the recurrent pattern is Nemesis'. The classic statement of this theme is by R. G. Moulton in *Shakespeare as a Dramatic Artist* (1885):

When Clarence perished it was the King who dealt the doom and the Queen's party who triumphed; the wheel of Nemesis goes round and the King's death follows the death of his victim, the Queen's kindred are naked to the vengeance of their enemies, and Hastings is left to exult. Again the wheel of Nemesis revolves, and Hastings at the moment of his highest exultation is hurled to destruction, while Buckingham stands by to point the moral with a gibe. Once more the wheel goes round, and Buckingham hears similar gibes addressed to himself and points the same moral in his own person.

The introduction of Queen Margaret into *Richard III* (although historically she has no part in the events with which it deals) has the effect of bringing out the underlying theme of the play. Rivers, Grey, Hastings, Buckingham – each of Richard's victims in turn recalls Margaret's curses and prophecies in I,3, and accepts his death as the working of fate. And if Margaret is the voice of Nemesis, Richard is its instrument; it is he who brings about the destruction of the house of York – and he is himself the final victim of Nemesis. As Moulton says:

Although the various Nemesis Actions have been carried on by their own motion and by the force of retribution as a principle of moral government, yet there is not one of them which reaches its goal without at some point of its course receiving an impetus from contact with Richard.

Richard is the source of movement to the whole drama, communicating his own energy through all parts. It is only fitting that the motive force to this system of nemeses should be itself a grand Nemesis Action, the *Life and Death,* or crime and retribution, *of Richard III* ... The finger of Nemesis has been pointing at him all his life and he has never seen it!

Nemesis is a concept of requital, of balance, of tit for tat. It is based on a conviction that beneath all the disorder there is a pattern of order and justice. This sense of justice balancing one scale against the other is echoed in so many of the striking phrases of the play: 'Plantagenet doth quit Plantagenet'; 'brother to brother, Blood to blood, self against self'; 'right for right' (which Dr Johnson paraphrased as 'Justice answering the claim of justice'); 'Wrong hath but wrong, and blame the due of blame'. It seems to colour much of the language of the play, with its repeated patterns of verse structure and much antithesis and balance within a single line. Further, one senses it in the structure of the play. Richard's wooing of Anne (I,2) is balanced by his wooing of Queen Elizabeth (IV,4); the dream of Clarence (I,4) by the dream of Richard (V,3); the prophecies of Margaret (I,3) by the prophecy of Henry VI (IV,2); the murder of the child Rutland, described as 'the most merciless [deed] that e'er was heard of' (I,3), by the murder of the child Princes, described as 'the most arch deed of piteous massacre That ever yet this land was guilty of' (IV,3).

## Atmosphere

The atmosphere of the play is an unusual mixture of light and shade, of vengeance and cruelty on the one hand, and of Richard's zest and gaiety in pursuing these on the other. In the background looms the Tower, and in the foreground bustles Richard, whose crimes we almost condone in our enjoyment of his dexterity.

The Tower of London seems to dominate the setting of the whole play, a grim symbol of repression and 'insulting tyranny'. It was the scene of Richard's first calculated murder, that of Henry VI, in his dreadful journey to the throne. At the beginning of the play we see Clarence on his way to the Tower, and Hastings just released from it. It is the scene of Clarence's murder. No sooner has Edward V arrived in London than he and the young Duke of York are despatched thither ('I do not like the Tower, of any place'). The Tower seems to brood ominously over the scene at

Hastings's house (III,2); it is mentioned four times ('And we will both together to the Tower, Where, we shall see, the boar will use us kindly'); and later Hastings's horse 'startled when he look'd upon the Tower'. It is the scene of the Council meeting; Richard and Buckingham meet the Mayor on the Tower walls; and in IV,1 members of the house of York try to visit the young princes there ('Pity, you ancient stones, those tender babes').

Again, the atmosphere of the play seems coloured with blood. The occurrences of this word in *Richard III* are almost too numerous to count; it is constantly on the lips of almost every character – both in the sense of bloodshed, and with its other meaning of kinsman fighting against kinsman ('brother to brother, Blood to blood, self against self'). From the introduction of the corpse of Henry VI ('Thou bloodless remnant of that royal blood') to the death of Richard himself ('The bloody dog is dead'), the word echoes through the play. Richard is described as 'One raised in blood, and one in blood established'. He himself says he is 'So far in blood that sin will pluck on sin'. And in the very last lines of the play Richmond prays that his country may be free from traitors,

That would reduce these bloody days again,
And make poor England weep in streams of blood.

These are only a few of the significant uses of the word.

In the almost complete absence of political order which the play reveals, men have become like animals preying on one another. This is emphasized by the frequent animal imagery in the play. Most of the animal images are applied to Richard himself, who is described by one character or another as a hedgehog, a toad, an 'elvish-mark'd, abortive, rooting hog', a cockatrice, a hell-hound, a carnal cur, a 'wretched, bloody and usurping boar', a tiger, a bottled spider and a 'poisonous bunch-back'd toad'. And his epitaph is 'The bloody dog is dead.'

The play also contains a considerable number of images from the theatre. It is as if the oppressive atmosphere is lightened by an indication that these characters are playing parts, parts which are thrust upon them by the ghastly tragedy in which they are performing, but that basic human nature is better than they can exemplify. The most brilliant and sparkling actor of all, of course, is Richard himself, a mercurial temperament, throwing himself with gusto, skill and gaiety into a succession of parts, but unconscious of his most significant role, cast by fate in the part of avenger in a tragedy of Nemesis.

## The moral atmosphere

It has been said that 'the artistic weakness of *Richard III* is that Shakespeare has chosen a potentially tragic situation for the creation of his first great comic character' (M. M. Reese, *The Cease of Majesty*). The situation is only potentially tragic, for it may be questioned whether the play is a tragedy at all. Certainly it would be wrong to consider it in the same light as we consider *King Lear* or *Hamlet* or *Macbeth*. *Richard III* has none of the tragic atmosphere of those later plays, where we are moved to pity and horror as we witness the struggle between good and evil, and see how man's helplessness springs from human character and how in the overcoming of evil much that is noble and glorious must suffer and be destroyed.

Many critics claim to have found a moral issue at the heart of the play. Coleridge said that Shakespeare 'here as in all his great parts, develops in a tone of sublime morality the dreadful consequences of placing the moral in subordination to the mere intellectual being'. Professor Dowden saw Richard as inverting the moral order of things and 'dashing himself to pieces against the laws of the world which he has outraged'.

But the characters in *Richard III* are rather too remote from normal human nature, and certainly too remote from any relevant concept of kingship, for the reader or spectator to feel closely involved in any moral issue. We feel no sympathy with either Richard or his victims in their deaths; the latter are for the most part despicable or weak or themselves eaten up by the lust for power, and Richard, with his wit, courage, charm and candour, provides us with excellent entertainment. He is like the Vice in the old morality plays (he is himself aware of the comparison – see III,1, 82–3): we know that he must eventually be banished but we enjoy his entertaining presence. We feel no admiration for Richmond; he appears to be invested with no compelling significance.

Above all, the pattern of Nemesis means that we have no sense of tragic waste; death is a just retribution. The struggle lacks 'inwardness'; we witness no harrowing conflicts in the soul of man; and we see no development in any of the characters in the course of the play. The only characters who face any kind of moral dilemma are the murderers of Clarence. It is instructive to compare *Richard III* in this respect with *Macbeth*, a play of Shakespeare's maturity which deals with a similar theme, but with full tragic significance.

# The characters

Even more strikingly than with *Hamlet*, the central character dominates the play. There is no character in *Richard III* whose stature is in any way comparable with that of Richard himself; and with the exception of Buckingham and Queen Margaret there is no other character of whom much need be said here.

This is not to say that the minor characters are not distinctly drawn. Even at the very beginning of his career Shakespeare was able to distinguish for us Edward V from the Duke of York, the first murderer from the second murderer, and even the first citizen from the second and third. But they are drawn in black and white, as it were; only Richard is in full colour.

## Richard

I am determined to prove a villain

Discussion of Richard must begin for us, as it did for Shakespeare, with his deformity. Richard often speaks of it and it is clear that it is a decisive factor in his attitude to the world. But he does not envy others their 'fair proportion'. He rejoices in his deformity because it makes him different from them; it marks him as unique, so that he treats other men's motives with contempt.

I have no brother, I am like no brother;
And this word 'love', which greybeards call divine,
Be resident in men like one another
And not in me: I am myself alone.
(*Henry VI, Part 3, V,6*)

In this respect he has much in common with the Machiavellian creations of Marlowe. His deformity supplies him with an incentive to prove that he is not only different from other men: he is superior to them. He has many qualities which, if directed to other ends, would be entirely admirable. It was this respect which caused Charles Lamb to write of 'the lofty genius, the man of vast capacity, the profound, the witty, the accomplished Richard'. He has great intelligence, which he applies to achieving his purpose, using the ambitions of others, like Hastings and Buckingham, to gain his own ends. His wit and his quick-thinking are evident in the way he parries Anne's objections, in the neatness with which he turns Margaret's curse against herself, and in the rapidity with which he seizes any opportunity for word-play. This in turn is an aspect of his gaiety, often hidden under a cloak of solemnity, as in his conversation with Clarence or his fooling of the Lord Mayor by pretending danger. It often reveals itself as disarming self-mockery:

Upon my life, she finds, although I cannot,
Myself to be a marvellous proper man.

His courage is undeniable. When battle comes he goes to it pell-mell, 'If not to heaven, then hand in hand to hell'; and on Bosworth field

The king enacts more wonders than a man,
Daring an[d] opposite to every danger.

He is a fine soldier, but he is also a polished courtier with a charm of presence. Lamb said that an actor playing the part must bring out the 'fine address, which was necessary to have betrayed the heart of Lady Anne'. And with this goes an artist's pride in his achievements. When he *has* conquered Anne we feel his glee:

Was ever woman in this humour woo'd?
Was ever woman in this humour won?

He is completely lacking in many of the meaner qualities of mankind: he has no fear, envy self-delusion or self-pity.

Unfortunately, however, he is completely lacking also in the finer qualities of mankind. He lacks 'humanity'. His mother says of him:

Tetchy and wayward was thy infancy;
Thy schooldays frightful, desperate, wild and furious;
Thy prime of manhood daring, bold, and venturous;
Thy age confirmed, proud, subtle, sly and bloody,
More mild, but yet more harmful, kind in hatred.

But of all this he is proud. Tear-falling pity dwells not in his eye, and to him conscience is but a word that cowards use.

Yet Richard pretends that he is a plain and harmless creature, free from all dissembling. Because he cannot flatter, he is hurt that others should misunderstand him. He is, he says, 'too childish-foolish for this world'. Nothing is farther from his thoughts than to be king: he would rather be a pedlar! He hates enmity and only desires all good men's love.

I do not know that Englishman alive
With whom my soul is any jot at odds
More than the infant that is born to-night:
I thank my God for my humility.

– and this after he has just arranged the murder of Clarence, his brother!

He is a consummate hypocrite, but he never deceives the audience, whom he takes into his confidence and to whom he tells all, in asides and explanatory soliloquies. From them he keeps no secrets and his villainy is quite unabashed. No sooner has he won the Lady Anne than he says, 'I'll have her, but I will not keep her long'; and when he has set the house of York by the ears he tells us:

I do the wrong, and first begin to brawl.
The secret mischiefs that I set abroach
I lay unto the grievous charge of others.

It is a feature of Richard's engaging candour that it is often accompanied by an air of mock-piety:

But then I sigh; and with a piece of scripture,
Tell them that God bids us do good for evil:
And thus I clothe my naked villainy
With old odd ends stolen forth of holy writ,
And seem a saint when most I play the devil.

And because his victims are for the most part mean and despicable we share his delight in his hoodwinking of them.

Richard holds us spellbound as a brilliant actor holds his audience, and he thoroughly enjoys his role and the power it gives him. He has a wonderful feeling for words and a subtle skill in using them. Even after she has been disillusioned, Anne has to acknowledge the power of Richard's 'honey words'. Combined with its persuasive force, Richard's language sometimes has a refreshing colloquial vigour, as when he says that he runs before his horse to market or that Edward must not die 'till George be pack'd with post-horse up to heaven'.

In the course of the play we see him throwing himself with gusto into a succession of parts: loving brother, impassioned wooer, wronged courtier, reluctant ruler, and so on. Moreover, he knows exactly the right dramatic moment at which to burst upon a scene:

Stay, you that bear the course . . . (I,2)
They do me wrong, and I will not endure it . . . (I,3)
I pray you all, tell me what they deserve . . . (III,4)

– and he knows exactly when to strike his blows: consider his timing of the announcement of the death of Clarence, the arrest of Rivers, Grey and Vaughan, and the arrest of Hastings at the Council meeting in the Tower.

It is debatable how far Richard's actions are motivated solely by ambition, by an overpowering desire for the throne. Comparing him with Bolingbroke in *Richard II*, Coleridge makes a significant remark: 'In Richard III the pride of intellect *makes use of ambition as the means;* in Bolingbroke the gratification of ambition is the end and talents are the means.' It is as though Richard were a tremendous force which must somehow release its pent-up energy. Since ordinary outlets are denied him, and since in any case he does not think in terms of right and wrong, his destructive energy is directed to manipulating the lives of those around him in order to obtain for himself the highest reward that he can conceive.

God take King Edward to his mercy,
And leave the world *for me to bustle in.*

We cannot but admire his audacity in attempting the impossible, whether it is gaining the crown or winning Anne as his wife ('What though I kill'd her husband and her father?"), and we cannot but share his delight when he succeeds.

Only towards the end does he begin to flag, and after he has gained the throne some of his power seems to leave him. He fails to win over Elizabeth as he had won over Anne. His orders to Ratcliffe and Catesby are confused. His outburst at the third messenger shows lack of his usual self-control. He confesses:

I have not that alacrity of spirit,
Nor cheer of mind, that I was wont to have.

His words as he awakes from his dream reveal deep psychological conflict, and a little later he says,

 Shadows to-night
Have struck more terror to the soul of Richard
Than can the substance of ten thousand soldiers.

But the old Richard soon reasserts itself. With a characteristic phrase ('Come, bustle, bustle!') he is soon busy again, applying his intelligence to the plan of battle, denying that conscience has any part in his make-up, refusing to let 'babbling dreams affright our souls', and addressing his army in a speech full of spirit. On the battlefield he 'enacts more wonders than a man'. Though his horse his killed under him, he continues to fight on foot, determined to find Richmond. They meet in a hand-to-hand combat and Richard is killed. 'The bloody dog is dead.'

Reader and spectator are content that this should be Richard's epitaph. But we cannot forget that we have been agreeably dazzled by his brilliance and his energy. What Lamb said of Shakespeare's villains is eminently true of Richard: 'We think not so much of the crimes which they commit as of the ambition, the aspiring spirit, the intellectual activity which prompts them to overleap the moral fences.'

## Buckingham

I can counterfeit the deep tragedian

It is Shakespeare's purpose to show Richard as a towering figure of evil and so at the beginning he must stand alone. Only later does Buckingham play his role as Richard's henchman, urged on by his own desire for greater power and position. At first he says little. He joins the rest in rounding on Margaret for the murder of Rutland, and when she curses the others in terrible words she delivers to Buckingham the warning that one day Richard 'shall split thy very heart with sorrow'. With smooth insincerity Buckingham professes amity with the Queen's kindred in words that are later to recoil upon him with a full measure of irony. At the end of this scene Richard and Buckingham are alone together for the first time. We sense an understanding between them: Buckingham is almost as much a dissembler as his master.

But, compared with Richard's, Buckingham's deceitfulness is a little amateurish. He lacks Richard's light touch. His words to the 'cloudly princes and heart-sorrowing peers' after the death of Edward are a little too unctuous, and he comes rather too quickly to his suggestion that the Prince of Wales should be brought to London with 'some little train'. It is clear that things will fall out the way Richard wants. After all, he is now Protector and he can afford to let Buckingham delude himself into believing that he is taking the initiative.

Richard now lets Buckingham have a long lead. At the Prince's arrival in London, Buckingham plays a bigger part. He takes it upon himself to administer a scathing rebuke over 'sanctuary children' to the Archbishop of Canterbury, joins with Richard in a somewhat condescending conversation with the young Princes, and tries to smooth over the Duke of York's jest at his uncle's deformity. At the end of the scene he makes the arrangements with Catesby for the sounding of Lord Hastings; but it is clear that he is putting into effect only what Richard has already planned, for Richard promises him the earldom of Hereford as a reward.

At the Council meeting at the Tower, Buckingham speaks more truly than he could possibly suspect when he says that he knows no more of Richard's mind than Ely does of his. Richard is merely making use of Buckingham to help in disposing of Hastings, who is likely to object to Richard's taking the throne, just as immediately afterwards he uses Buckingham to help in deceiving the Lord Mayor and citizens. It is now that Buckingham seems to adopt his master's very voice:

> Ghastly looks
> Are at my service, like enforced smiles;
> And both are ready in their offices,
> At any time, to grace my stratagems;

and to suggest an idea (the 'two churchmen') that Richard had already put into his head. Buckingham plays his part with skill in the pantomime which follows, and each rhetorical exaggeration, each calculated pause, shows how much he is learning from Richard. But the latter, as John Palmer says, 'has the natural contempt of an original mind for a reproduction'. When Richard 'plays the touch' to find out whether Buckingham will support him in the murder of the young Princes, Buckingham hesitates, and that hesitation is his undoing. He thought he could go along with Richard on his own terms and set his own limits. But in a career of crime there can be no limited liability, and Buckingham is unceremoniously discarded and left to ponder Richard's ingratitude.

We last see him, after his failure to raise an army and join Richmond, facing execution at Salisbury and acknowledging the justice of his fate. The scales have fallen from the eyes of princely Buckingham.

## Margaret

Remember Margaret was a prophetess

Shakespeare had already told the whole story of this remarkable woman, of her love, her treachery and her tyranny, in the three parts of *Henry VI*. In defiance of historical accuracy he introduces her into *Richard III*. Here she plays no part in the plot and appears in only two scenes, but by making her a Chorus to the events of the play, the voice of Nemesis, Shakespeare emphasizes the theme of the play. (See 'Theme and structure', p.74.)

She has been called 'the terrible spirit of this age of strife' (E. Dowden) and 'the incarnate Fury of the Civil Wars' (Stopford A. Brooke), and, indeed, there is something almost inhuman about her. She is greeted at her entrance with phrases like 'foul, wrinkled witch' and 'hateful wither'd hag'. She directs her harsh invective mainly on Richard, whom she calls a devil, a cacodemon whose real kingdom is Hell. He and the other characters turn their hatred on her, especially for the murder of Rutland, before she utters her curses – on Edward IV, the Prince of Wales, Queen Elizabeth, Rivers, Dorset, Hastings, Buckingham and Richard. These curses seem to reverberate through the rest of the play. At Pomfret Castle, Rivers and Grey recall her words and pray that her curses on Hastings, Buckingham and Richard may be fulfilled. In the Tower Hastings recalls her words and prophesies Richard's doom. At Salisbury, Buckingham recalls her words and imagines the souls of the previous victims mocking his destruction.

Margaret's second and final appearance is at the very time when Richard begins to taste success turning bitter, realizing that his kingdom 'stands on brittle glass' and that he must embark on further evil. Margaret provides a fitting comment on the situation:

So, now prosperity begins to mellow
And drop into the rotten mouth of death.
Here in these confines slily have I lurk'd
To watch the waning of mine enemies.
A dire induction am I witness to,
And will to France, hoping the consequence
Will prove as bitter, black, and tragical.

She has no compassion for the sorrows of Queen Elizabeth and the Duchess of York. Indeed, she rejoices at them, believing that they are merely a return for the sorrows she has been made to suffer by the house of York. But the end she prophesied is near:

   I am hungry for revenge,
And now I cloy me with beholding it . . .
Earth gapes, hell burns, fiends roar, saints pray,
To have him suddenly convey'd from hence.
Cancel his bond of life, dear God! I pray,
That I may live and say, The dog is dead.

After teaching the other two to curse, Margaret leaves the play. She does not live to say, 'The dog is dead'. The words are said for her by Richmond. She is mentioned for the last time by Buckingham, Richard's last and greatest victim  Richard has fulfilled the role for which Margaret cast him, the avenger on whom is taken the final revenge. Bosworth Field follows immediately. It only remains for Richmond to bring down the curtain.

## Other characters

*Lord Hastings* Richard's early ally is motivated by his hatred of the Queen's faction, whom he holds responsible for his imprisonment at the beginning of the play, and when Rivers, Vaughan and Grey are executed he laughs 'to look upon their tragedy'. He helps Richard to become Lord Protector but opposes his claim to the crown. His character is tainted by his liaison with Mistress Shore. He rejects Stanley's advice to fly from Richard's displeasure and in his blind self-confidence he believes that 'nothing can proceed that toucheth us'. When, on his way to the council meeting, he encounters the pursuivant and the priest, representing the worlds of temporal and spiritual affairs, he is unaware that they are what Holinshed called 'fore-tokens of imminent misfortune', but at that meeting he quickly realizes the folly of his blind trust in 'mortal men' and in one man in particular. Like Buckingham, he is a tool that Richard discards when it suits him.

*Clarence* Like so many other characters in this play, 'false, fleeting, perjur'd Clarence' is saddled with the heavy burden of his previous history. His treachery and his death present another variation on the theme of Nemesis. There is much pathos in his account of his dream and 'the tempest' in his soul, yet together with the fine poetry Shakespeare provides enough historical reference (to Warwick, Prince Edward and 'the field by Tewkesbury') for us to be fully aware of Clarence's treachery.

*King Edward* Edward appears in only one scene (II,1) and in the next his wife and mother vie with each other in the rhetoric by which they mourn his death. Richard regards the King's illness as a consequence of his self-indulgence and loose living but for audience and readers his belief that he has reconciled the fac-tious nobles and his remorse at the death of Clarence have an air of piety.

*Queen Elizabeth* From the beginning Elizabeth, her children and her brothers stand in the way of Richard's designs. The target for his 'blunt upbraidings and bitter scoffs', she finds 'small joy in being England's queen'. After Edward's death, her brother and her son (Earl Rivers and Lord Grey), and her two youngest children (the Prince of Wales and the Duke of York) are all murdered at Richard's command. She has much to lament and even Queen Margaret, who calls her 'poor shadow, painted queen' and 'queen of sad mischance', acknowledges this and lists her misfortunes at some length in IV,4. Yet after the long interview with Richard, who calls her 'shallow, changing woman' and tries to persuade her to woo her daughter for him, she finally outwits him — her daughter eventually marries Richmond.

*Duchess of York:* Like Margaret and Elizabeth, the Duchess of York has much cause for lamentation and joins them in their maledictory chorus in IV,4. Her easy chatter with the children of Clarence (II,2) and the young Duke of York (II,4) is very different from her scenes with Richard. She has a profound understanding of her son; she calls him a toad and a cockatrice, and applies to him a whole array of adjectives that range from wayward and wild to subtle, sly and bloody.

*Lady Anne* Succumbing to Richard's honeyed words, Anne provides him with his first triumph in the play. Before they meet she prays that, if he marries, his wife may have a miserable life; and this, as Richard's queen and 'the subject of mine own soul's curse', she later has to endure. She does not appear after IV,1. Richard puts about the rumour that she is 'grievous sick' and in IV,3 he tells us that she has 'bid the world good night'.

*Earl of Richmond* Of Richmond almost all that can be said is that he is required by the plot and by history. He twice addresses his troops, speaking over and over again 'in God's name', and at Bosworth Field he has the blessing of the ghosts of Richard's victims. When good triumphs over evil and 'the bloody dog is dead', Richmond promises that his marriage with Elizabeth's daughter will unite the houses of York and Lancaster in peace and prosperity.

*Lord Stanley (Earl of Derby)* As a character in the play Stanley, ambiguous and evasive (see especially IV,4), is bound to appear somewhat unreal, for his function too is completely determined by history. He is the stepfather of Richmond and his treachery to Richard must be made to appear what it is not.

# Style

## Language

*Richard III* is one of Shakespeare's very earliest plays. Its language is that of a young writer who seems at times to be almost too easily fascinated by the artifice of language, so that often we feel a straining after effect. It has been described as 'a highly mannered rhetorical style, extravagant in utterance, with many appeals and exclamations' (E. K. Chambers).

There are passages which suffer from compression of the thought (e.g. I,3,63–8; I,3,274–8; II,3,12–15; IV,4,26–8) or from Shakespeare's inability to resist an antithesis (e.g. I,2,75–80; IV,4,16). Words are piled up in extended parallels:

Bold, quick, ingenious, forward, capable (III,1,155)
Untainted, unexamin'd, free, at liberty (III,6,9).

There is an unusually large number of striking compounds – e.g. 'elvish-marked' (I,3,228), 'heart-sorrowing' (II,2,112), 'deep-revolving' (IV,2,42), 'tear-falling' (IV,2,65) – and doublets like 'childish-foolish' (I,3,142), 'senseless-obstinate' (III,1,44) and 'peevish-fond' (IV,4,417).

An important feature of the style of the play is Shakespeare's trick of playing with the patterns of a phrase or the repetition of a name. With Richard this is a sign of his quick-wittedness (e.g. I,2,140–147), and with the lamenting women a symptom of their overwrought emotion (e.g. II,2,71–85; IV,4,40–46). There are also three extended examples of dialogue in *sticomythia* (see note p.15), a device which the early Elizabethan dramatists adopted from classical drama and which Richard himself describes on one occasion as 'this keen encounter of our wits'. See I, 2, 68–88; IV, 4, 212–19; IV, 4, 343-67.

Many of the images (what the Elizabethans would have called 'conceits' (see *Literary terms*, p.15), are of a fantastic, far-fetched kind, forced and unnatural (e.g. II,2,67–70 and IV,4,127–9), very different from strikingly beautiful lines like:

the blind cave of eternal night (V,3, 62)

and

> the swallowing gulf
> Of dark forgetfulness and deep oblivion (III,7,127–8)

or the fierce invective of phrases like 'bunch-back'd toad' (I,3,246) and 'bottled spider' (IV,4,81).

Richard's own manner of speech often adds a further element to the play's considerable variety of styles with the colloquial vigour of expressions like 'bustle' (I,1,152), 'butt-end' (II,2,110), 'hoyday' (IV,4,460) and 'frank'd up for fatting' (I,3,313).

## Verse

The greater part of the play is written in blank verse. Even the dialogue of the citizens in II,3 and the scrivener in III,6 is written in verse, since it is felt to have a special significance. Clarence's murderers, however, speak in prose at first, but after Clarence wakes their speeches are in verse to mark the heightened emotional level of the rest of the scene.

Rhyming lines are few and are confined to three or four special uses. Rhyme often marks the end of a scene or of an episode (see the list of examples on p.10), and is sometimes used at the end of an important speech (e.g. IV,4,195–6), especially if this coincides with a character's exit. Rhyme is occasionally used to emphasize a statement (e.g. I,1,55–9; IV,4,15–16,20–21, 24–5) or to give point to an 'aside' (e.g. III,1,94). Some of the lines spoken by the Ghosts rhyme, and the speech of Buckingham's Ghost (the climax of this episode) ends with three rhyming couplets.

## Imagery

Very often with Shakespeare the tone of a play is set by groups of metaphors which are drawn from particular areas and which recur throughout the play. This is certainly true of *Richard III*. Attention has already been drawn to the frequent animal imagery (p.77).

There is an unusually large number of images from trees, often signifying the royal house with many branches, sometimes with withered roots and leaves, and plants with 'unblown flowers'. Note the references to herbs and weeds in the conversations with the young Duke of York (II,4 and III,1). All these images suggest the contrast between natural order on the one hand and decay or premature cropping on the other.

*Richard III* has many images which are connected with plays and actors and which suggest that the characters whose actions we are witnessing are mere dissemblers and hypocrites. We have, for example, 'scene of rude impatience . . . act of tragic violence' (II,2,38–9) and there are references to 'plots' and 'inductions' and 'tragedies'. Buckingham tells Richard (III,4,26–7):

'Had you not come upon your cue, my lord,
William Lord Hastings had pronounc'd your part'

and in the next scene boasts that he can 'counterfeit the deep tragedian (III,5,5). Margaret says that Elizabeth merely plays a part in 'a direful pageant' (IV,4,85). The most consummate actor of all is Richard himself, of course, and he delights in playing a part that is at the same time both wicked and winning:

'Thus, like the formal Vice, Iniquity,
I moralize two meanings in one word' (III,1,82–3).

(See also, under 'Atmosphere', p.76.)

The extremes of moral conduct shown by so many of the characters in the play seem to be underlined by the unusually frequent use of religious terms like heaven, hell, angel, devil, saint and above all the words 'God' and 'conscience', and E. A. J. Honigmann has drawn attention to 'the never-ending procession of churchmen across the stage'. All these elements provide a wider backcloth against which Richard's evil (with his *false* piety) is shown up for what it is – and for what he knows it to be:

'And thus I clothe my naked villainy
With odd old ends stol'n forth of Holy Writ,
And seem a saint, when most I play the devil' (I,3,336–8)


**Dramatic irony**

In *Richard III* Shakespeare makes full use of dramatic irony (see note, p.15). This is a most effective trick in writing for the theatre, especially in a play which involves so much plotting and dissembling and so many examples of the reversal of men's fortunes. Some examples of dramatic irony are Anne's curse on Richard, 'If ever he have wife . . .' (I,2,26–8); Buckingham's promise to Queen Elizabeth to 'cherish you and yours' (II,1,36); almost all of III,1, and most of what Hastings says in III,2. Perhaps the most subtle example, considering the manner of Clarence's death, is Richard's remark to him (I,1,49–50):

'O, belike his Majesty hath some intent
That you should be new-christen'd in the Tower.'

# General questions

**Note style answer**

**1** What do the women in *Richard III* contribute to the interest of the play?

For a history play *Richard III* has unusually large and important parts for women characters.

*Relevant scenes* I,2 – Richard woos *Lady Anne;* IV,1 – she recalls this meeting, her curse and her misery as Richard's wife; IV,3 – Anne dies and Richard plans to woo Elizabeth. I,3 – Richard quarrels with *the Queen* and her relatives, and *Queen Margaret* prophesies vengeance on Yorkists and Woodvilles; IV,4 – Queen Margaret exults in the fulfilment of her prophecies, and Queen Elizabeth and the *Duchess of York* (his mother) join her in cursing Richard; II,2 – a chorus of lamentation by the Queen and the Duchess of York. IV,1 – Queen Elizabeth, the Duchess of York and Queen Anne are refused admission to the Tower; IV,4 – after the chorus of lamentation and curses Richard wants Queen Elizabeth to woo her daughter for him.

The women's encounters with Richard serve to bring out aspects of his character: Anne – his personal charm and (later) his callousness; Queen Elizabeth – his cunning strategies; Margaret – his history of violence; Duchess of York – his ruthlessness. They add a depth of history (from them we learn much of the background of earlier events) and pathos. Queen Margaret is especially important as a Chorus, emphasizing the theme of Nemesis, and most of Richard's victims remember her at their deaths. The scenes of lamentation, in very formal verse, add an important sense of ritual to the play.

**2** How far does *Richard III* cater for the same tastes as a thriller?

**3** Discuss Shakespeare's interpretation of the historical events with which the play deals.

**4** 'Richard is a consummate actor' (E. K. Chambers). Discuss and illustrate.

**5** What other feelings do we have about Richard besides horror at his evil-doing?

**6** 'Shakespeare has succeeded in throwing a halo of poetry around this tiger in human shape' (George Brandes). Discuss.

**7** 'Richard is not a gloomy villain' (E. Dowden). Illustrate the lighter side of Richard's character by close reference to the play.

**8** 'In some places Shakespeare makes Richard a monster; in others he keeps him human' (E. M. W. Tillyard). Illustrate these two aspects of the portrayal of Richard and discuss Shakespeare's purpose in adopting this method.

**9** 'Richard's character does not grow upon us; from the first it is complete' (E. Dowden). Is this a weakness of Shakespeare's portrayal of his main character? By what other means does he maintain our interest in Richard?

**10** 'Richard thinks he makes and guides the storm in which so many lives are shipwrecked. He is really the chief victim of the storm, driven from shoal to shoal, till he is wrecked inevitably' (Stopford A. Brooke). Discuss.

**11** 'The downfall of Richard satisfies us in three ways: it is historically true, dramatically effective, and morally fitting.' Discuss and illustrate.

**12** What does the character of Buckingham contribute to the interest of the play?

**13** 'Nothing can be finer than this knitting of all the avenging forces round the supernatural image of Margaret' (Stopford A. Brooke). Discuss.

**14** 'Through her curses Margaret unwittingly creates the unity of the land she has so terribly injured' (E. M. W. Tillyard). Discuss and illustrate.

**15** 'The suffering of Richard's victims fails to move us.' Discuss.

**16** Discuss and illustrate the part played in *Richard III* by the ordinary people at the time.

**17** 'The real interest of the play is not historical at all: *Richard III* is a study of the evil man.' Discuss.

**18** '*Richard III* is not rightly tragedy, but melodrama; the melodrama of genius, yet all the more melodrama for that' (J. Dover Wilson). Discuss.

**19** 'The artistic weakness of *Richard III* is that Shakespeare has chosen a potentially tragic situation for the creation of his first great comic character' (M. M. Reese). Discuss.

**20** What indications do you find in the play of pity and humanity which act as a foil to the cruelty and harshness?

**21** Discuss and illustrate the use of dramatic irony in the play.

**22** Discuss and illustrate the use which Shakespeare makes of soliloquy in *Richard III*.

**23** Discuss the imagery of the play and show what it contributes to the atmosphere.

**24** Why do you think that *Richard III* has always been a popular play?

# Further reading

The student who wishes to know more of the historical events to which Shakespeare's play refers will find highly readable and reliable accounts of the period in Sir Winston Churchill's *A History of the English-Speaking Peoples*, Volume I, Book III ('The End of the Feudal Age') (Cassell 1956; paperback edition 1962) and in *Lancastrians, Yorkists and Henry VII* by S. B. Chrimes (Macmillan 1964). The connection between Shakespeare's plays and history is dealt with in *Shakespeare's English Kings: history, chronicle and drama* by Peter Saccio (OUP 1977).

Studies of the historical Richard III tend to be either strongly in favour, like Paul Murray Kendall's *Richard III* (George Allen & Unwin 1955; Cardinal paperback 1973), or violently opposed, like Desmond Seward's *Richard III: England's Black Legend* (Country Life 1983). A balanced and very readable account of Richard's reign is Giles St Aubyn's *The Year of Three Kings* (Collins 1983).

This study aid follows the text of the Arden Shakespeare, edited by Antony Hammond (Methuen 1981). Other important editions are the New Shakespeare, edited by J. Dover Wilson (CUP 1954), the New Clarendon Shakespeare, edited by R. E. C. Houghton (OUP 1965), and the New Penguin Shakespeare, edited by E. A. J. Honigmann (Penguin Books 1968).

The following critical works contain material on *Richard III* and will prove helpful for advanced study.

*Shakespeare, a survey* by E. K. Chambers (Sidgwick & Jackson 1925; Pelican Books 1964)

*Shakespeare as a Dramatic Artist* by R. G. Moulton (Clarendon Press 1893; Dover Publications 1966)

*Political Characters of Shakespeare* by John Palmer (Macmillan 1945; paperback edition, *Political and Comic Characters of Shakespeare*, 1962)

*The Cease of Majesty, a study of Shakespeare's History Plays* by M. M. Reese (Arnold 1961)

*Shakespeare's History Plays* by E. M. W. Tillyard (Chatto & Windus 1944; Peregrine Books 1962)

*Angel with Horns* by A. P. Rossiter (Longmans 1961; paperback edition 1970)

Several works of fiction have been based upon the events of Richard's reign. The following are the most important.

*Under the Hog* by Patrick Carleton (Rich & Cowan 1937; Sphere Books 1973)

*Crouchback* by Carola Oman (Hodder & Stoughton 1929)

*The Daughter of Time* by Josephine Tey (Peter Davies 1951; Penguin Books 1954)

*The Sunne in Splendour* by Sharon Penman (Macmillan 1983; Penguin Books 1984)

# Pan study aids Titles published in the Brodie's Notes series

**Jane Austen** Emma Mansfield Park Northanger Abbey Persuasion
Pride and Prejudice

**Geoffrey Chaucer (parallel texts editions)** The Franklin's Tale
The Knight's Tale The Miller's Tale The Nun's Priest's Tale
The Pardoner's Tale Prologue to the Canterbury Tales
The Wife of Bath's Tale

**Joseph Conrad** The Nigger of the Narcissus & Youth The Secret Agent

**Charles Dickens** Bleak House David Copperfield Dombey and Son
Great Expectations Hard Times Little Dorrit Oliver Twist
Our Mutual Friend A Tale of Two Cities

**George Eliot** Middlemarch The Mill on the Floss Silas Marner

**E. M. Forster** Howards End A Passage to India
Where Angels Fear to Tread

**William Golding** Lord of the Flies The Spire

**Graham Greene** Brighton Rock The Power and the Glory
The Quiet American

**Thomas Hardy** Chosen Poems of Thomas Hardy
Far from the Madding Crowd Jude the Obscure
The Mayor of Casterbridge Return of the Native
Tess of the d'Urbervilles The Trumpet-Major

**L. P. Hartley** The Go-Between The Shrimp and the Anemone

**Laurie Lee** As I Walked out One Midsummer Morning
Cider with Rosie

**Christopher Marlowe** Doctor Faustus Edward the Second

**John Milton** A Choice of Milton's Verse Comus and Samson
Agonistes Paradise Lost I, II

**Sean O'Casey** Juno and the Paycock
The Shadow of a Gunman and the Plough and the Stars

**George Orwell** Animal Farm 1984

**William Shakespeare** Antony and Cleopatra As You Like It
Coriolanus Hamlet Henry IV (Part 1) Henry IV (Part 2) Henry V
Julius Caesar King Lear Love's Labour's Lost Macbeth Measure for
Measure The Merchant of Venice A Midsummer Night's Dream
Much Ado about Nothing Othello Richard II Richard III Romeo and
Juliet The Sonnets The Taming of the Shrew The Tempest Twelfth
Night The Winter's Tale

# Pan study aids

Published jointly by Heinemann Educational Books and Pan Books

Pan Study Aids is a major new series developed to help school and college students prepare for examinations. All the authors are experienced teachers/examiners at O level, School Certificate and equivalent examinations and authors of textbooks used in schools and colleges worldwide

Each volume in the series:
- explains its subject and covers clearly and concisely and with excellent illustrations the essential points of the syllabus, drawing attention to common areas of difficulty and to areas which carry most marks in the exam

- gives guidance on how to plan revision, and prepare for the exam, outlining what examiners are looking for

- provides practice by including typical exam questions and exercises

Titles available: Physics, Chemistry, Maths, Human Biology, English Language, Geography 1 & 2, Economics, Commerce, Accounts and Book-keeping, British Government and Politics, History 1 & 2, Effective Study Skills, French, German, Spanish, Sociology